THE BREAD MACHINE COOKBOOK FOR BEGINNERS:

Easy-to-Follow Guide for Fast and Delicious Recipes. Quick-Easy Baked Homemade Bread: Buns, Snacks, Loaves, Gluten-free and pizza Dough

THE BREAD MACHINE COOKBOOK FOR BEGINNERS:

© Copyright 2020 - All rights reserved.

The content contained within this book may not be reproduced, duplicated or transmitted without direct written permission from the author or the publisher. Under no circumstances will any blame or legal responsibility be held against the publisher, or author, for any damages, reparation, or monetary loss due to the information contained within this book. Either directly or indirectly.

Legal Notice:

This book is copyright protected. This book is only for personal use. You cannot amend, distribute, sell, use, quote or paraphrase any part, or the content within this book, without the consent of the author or publisher.

Disclaimer Notice:

Please note the information contained within this document is for educational and entertainment purposes only. All effort has been executed to present accurate, up to date, and reliable, complete information. No warranties of any kind are declared or implied. Readers acknowledge that the author is not engaging in the rendering of legal, financial, medical or professional advice. The content within this book has been derived from various sources. Please consult a licensed professional before attempting any techniques outlined in this book.

By reading this document, the reader agrees that under no circumstances is the author responsible for any losses, direct or indirect, which are incurred as a result of the use of information contained within this document, including, but not limited to, errors, omissions, or inaccuracies.

THE BREAD MACHINE COOKBOOK FOR BEGINNERS:

Table of Contents

INTRODUCTION 8

CHAPTER 1: BENEFITS AND HOW TO USE BREAD MAKER 10
- Benefits of Bread Machine 10
- How to Use a Bread Machine 11

CHAPTER 2: TROUBLESHOOTING: PROBLEM AND SOLUTION 14

CHAPTER 3: HOW TO MAINTAIN SOURDOUGH STARTER 16
- Using A Starter 16
- Maintaining A Starter 16

CHAPTER 4: SELECTING THE RIGHT KIND OF YEAST 18

CHAPTER 5: WHITE BREAD 20
1. Amish Bread 20
2. Apricot Oat Bread 20
3. Basic White Bread 21
4. Basil and Sundried Tomato Bread 21
5. Baxi's White Bread 22
6. Best Bread Machine Bread 23
7. Buttermilk White Bread 23
8. Cinnamon Swirl Bread 24
9. Cottage Cheese Bread 25
10. Yeasted Cornbread 25
11. Homemade Wonderful Bread 26
12. Honey White Bread 26
13. Jos Rosemary Bread 27
14. Light Oat Bread 27
15. Alligator Animal Italian Bread 28

CHAPTER 6: WHOLEGRAIN BREAD 30
16. Seven-Grain Bread 30
17. Seven-Grain Oat Molasses Bread 30
18. Eight-Grain Bread 31
19. Ten Grain Bread 32
20. Bread Machine Multigrain Loaf 32
21. Whole-Grain Sesame Bread 33
22. Spent Grain Wheat Bread 33
23. Seven-Grain Millet Bread 34
24. Seven Grain Bread II 34
25. Multigrain Raisin Bread 35

CHAPTER 7: RYE BREAD 36
26. Basic Rye Bread 36
27. Buttermilk Rye Bread 36
28. Caraway Rye Bread 37
29. Chai Cake 38
30. Danish Rugbrod 38
31. Danish Spiced Rye Bread 39
32. Health Dynamics Rye Bread 40
33. Montana Russian Black Bread 41
34. Mustard Wheat Rye Sandwich Bread ... 42
35. New York Rye Bread 42

CHAPTER 8: VEGETABLE BREADS 44
36. Healthy Celery Loaf 44
37. Broccoli and Cauliflower Bread 45
38. Zucchini Herbed Bread 45
39. Potato Bread 46
40. Golden Potato Bread 47
41. Onion Potato Bread 48
42. Spinach Bread 48
43. Curd Bread 49
44. Curvy Carrot Bread 50
45. Potato Rosemary Bread with Honey 50
46. Beetroot Prune Bread 51
47. Sun Vegetable Bread 52
48. Tomato Onion Bread 52
49. Tomato Bread 53
50. Curd Onion Bread with Sesame Seeds .. 54
51. Zucchini Carrot Bread 54
52. Olive Bread with Italian Herbs 55
53. French Cheese Onion Bread 56
54. Italian Onion Bread 57
55. Carrot Oat Bread 57

CHAPTER 9: CHEESE BREAD 59
56. Cream Cheese Rolls 59
57. Cheesy Garlic Bread 60
58. Cheese Blend Bread 60
59. Parmesan Italian Bread 61
60. Cheese Spinach Crackers 62
61. Cheesy Keto Sesame Bread 63
62. Ricotta Bread 63
63. American Cheese Beer Bread 64

| 64. | Bacon Jalapeño Cheesy Bread .... 65 |
| 65. | Cheese Jalapeno Bread............................. 66 |

CHAPTER 10: SAVORY BREADS 67

66.	Cream Cheese Bread 67
67.	Lemon Poppy Seed Bread 67
68.	Cauliflower and Garlic Bread 68
69.	Almond Meal Bread 69
70.	Macadamia Nut Bread 69
71.	3-Seed Bread 70
72.	Cumin Bread 71
73.	Basic Rosemary Bread 71
74.	Sesame and Flax Seed Bread 72
75.	Dill and Cheddar Bread 73

CHAPTER 11: MEAT BREAD 74

76.	French Ham Bread 74
77.	Chicken Bread 75
78.	Onion Bacon Bread 75
79.	Beef and Parmesan Bread 76
80.	Bacon and Walnuts Rye Bread 77
81.	Turkey Breast Bread.................................. 78
82.	Bread with Chicken, Apricots, and Raisins..... 79
83.	Bread with Beef and Hazelnuts 80
84.	Bread with Ham and Sausages 81
85.	Bread with Sausages and Celery 81

CHAPTER 12: GRAIN, SEED AND NUT BREAD...... 83

86.	Oat Bread 83
87.	Whole-Wheat Bread 84
88.	Golden Corn Bread 84
89.	Oatmeal Bread... 85
90.	Corn, Poppy Seeds, and Sour Cream Bread.... 86
91.	Grump's Special Bread.............................. 87
92.	Butter Honey Wheat Bread 87
93.	Buttermilk Wheat Bread 88
94.	Cracked Wheat Bread 88
95.	Flax and Sunflower Seed Bread................. 89
96.	High Flavor Bran Bread 90
97.	Honey and Flaxseed Bread 90
98.	Honey Whole Wheat Bread 91
99.	Maple Whole Wheat Bread 91
100.	Oat and Honey Bread 92

101.	Nutty Bread 93
102.	Multi-Seed Bread 93
103.	Barley Bread 94
104.	Walnut Bread 94
105.	Peanut Butter Bread 95

CHAPTER 13: HERBED AND SPICE BREAD........... 97

106.	Original Italian Herb Bread 97
107.	Aromatic Lavender Bread..................... 98
108.	Cinnamon & Dried Fruits Bread........... 98
109.	Herbal Garlic Cream Cheese Delight 99
110.	Oregano Mozza-Cheese Bread 100
111.	Cumin Tossed Fancy Bread................. 100
112.	Potato Rosemary Loaf 101
113.	Honey Lavender Bread....................... 102
114.	Cinnamon Bread................................ 102
115.	Lavender Buttermilk Bread 103
116.	Cajun Bread 104
117.	Turmeric Bread 104
118.	Rosemary Cranberry Pecan Bread...... 105
119.	Sesame French Bread......................... 106
120.	Saffron Tomato Bread 106
121.	Cracked Black Pepper Bread 107
122.	Garlic, Herb, and Cheese Bread........... 108
123.	Onion Bread....................................... 108
124.	Spiced Cauliflower Buns 109
125.	Rosemary & Garlic Coconut Flour Bread 110

CHAPTER 14: GLUTEN-FREE BREAD 111

126.	Gluten-Free Simple Sandwich Bread .. 111
127.	Gluten-Free Chia Bread 112
128.	Gluten-Free Brown Bread 112
129.	Easy Gluten-Free, Dairy-Free Bread ... 113
130.	Gluten-Free Sourdough Bread 114
131.	Gluten-Free Crusty Boule Bread 115
132.	Gluten-Free Potato Bread 115
133.	Gluten-Free Sorghum Bread Recipe ... 116
134.	Gluten-Free Paleo Bread................... 117
135.	Gluten-Free Oat & Honey Bread 118
136.	Gluten-Free Cinnamon Raisin Bread .. 118
137.	Gluten-Free Pumpkin Pie Bread......... 119
138.	Gluten-Free Pizza Crust 120
139.	Gluten-Free Whole Grain Bread........ 121
140.	Gluten-Free Pull-Apart Rolls 122

CHAPTER 15: BREAKFAST, FRUIT AND CHOCOLATE BREAD 123

141. English Muffin Bread 123
142. Cranberry Orange Breakfast Bread 124
143. Buttermilk Honey Bread 124
144. Whole Wheat Breakfast Bread 125
145. Cinnamon-Raisin Bread 126
146. Butter Bread Rolls 126
147. Cranberry & Golden Raisin Bread 127
148. Chocolate Cherry Bread 128
149. Chocolate Orange Bread 128
150. Almond Chocolate Chip Bread 129
151. Walnut Cocoa Bread 130
152. Mexican Chocolate Bread 130
153. Banana Chocolate Chip Bread 131
154. Chocolate Chip Bread 132
155. Sunny Delight Loaf 132
156. Dark Rye Loaf 133
157. Paradise Bread 134
158. Bran Packed Healthy Bread 135
159. Orange Walnut Candied Loaf 135
160. Orchard's Dream Bread 136
161. Sesame Seeds & Onion Bread 136
162. Multigrain Bread with Honey 137
163. Rice Bread 138
164. Crunchy Wheat Herbed Bread 138
165. Flower Power Bread 139

CHAPTER 16: INTERNATIONAL BREAD, PIZZA AND FOCACCIA 140

166. German Pumpernickel Bread 140
167. European Black Bread 141
168. French Baguettes 141
169. Italian Bread 142
170. Portuguese Sweet Bread 143
171. Pita Bread 143
172. Syrian Bread 144
173. Sour Cream Chive Bread 145
174. Swedish Cardamom Bread 145
175. Ethiopian Milk and Honey Bread 146
176. Fiji Sweet Potato Bread 147
177. Italian Panettone 147
178. Bread of the Dead (Pan de Muertos) .. 148
179. Mexican Sweet Bread 149
180. Challah 150
181. Russian Black Bread 150
182. Russian Rye Bread 151
183. Portuguese Corn Bread 152
184. Amish Wheat Bread 152
185. British Hot Cross Buns 153
186. Hawaiian Bread 154
187. Greek Easter Bread 154
188. Sweet Potato Bread with Honey 155
189. Za'atar Bread 156
190. Bread Machine Pizza Dough 156
191. Perfect Thin Crust Pizza Dough 157
192. Pizza Crust 158
193. Rustic Pizza Bread 158
194. Red Pesto Focaccia 159
195. Hummus Focaccia 160
196. Porcini Focaccia 161
197. Potato Caraway Focaccia 162
198. Rosemary Mustard Focaccia 163
199. Green Peppercorn Focaccia 164
200. Roasted Garlic and Olive Focaccia 165

CONCLUSION **167**

RECIPES INDEX **169**

THE BREAD MACHINE COOKBOOK FOR BEGINNERS:

Introduction

Bread has existed for more than 35,000 years, proof of which can be found baked into pottery and in ancient caves worldwide. Archaeological evidence suggests that a wheat-based diet became a cornerstone of human existence nearly 10,000 years ago, and wheat remains the preferred grain to this day.

The first bread recipes appear around 1,500 BC in Egyptian cookbooks, and by the 7th century AD in Greece. The Roman invasion of Egypt, around 200 BC, led to the spread of flatbread across Europe, where it was adopted in all its forms and became a staple food across the continent, especially in Italy.

In the fourth century AD, when the Huns conquered Italy's northern part, the bread-baking profession became an exclusively male domain. When southern Italy was brought under Christian rule by the Normans in the late 11th century, the bread-baking secrets were brought to France, which today boasts some of the world's most incredible bakers. Baking was, and still is, an art not easily mastered, and the bread lessons handed down from generation to generation were passed on in the guarded ways only time-proven bakers could do.

When Napoleon conquered the Italian peninsula in the early 1800s, the bread-baking industry was turned on its head and gradually moved south. Today, Italy is credited with being the largest bread-baking nation globally, but France remains the bread capital of Europe. However, advances in food production in the mid-1900s led to a ban on naturally leavened bread that is still in effect today throughout Europe, excluding a few small markets, where loaves must be labeled as such.

Throughout the 20th century, bread baking remained the domain of home-made artisanal bakeries that produced hundreds if not thousands of different types of bread, all unique and distinct from others, and known by their specific names' baguette, ciabatta, baton, and fougasse.

The domestication of wheat, and from there to bread, is a long, arduous, and intriguing path, as are practically all of man's discoveries. Bread has been an integral part of the diet of most cultures throughout history. It has been used as currency and barter, as food for religious rituals, and as a way of preserving grains in storage. Although today, it has mostly been replaced by the more convenient method of keeping through bottling, it still holds a place in most people's hearts.

But bread isn't that simple. It's not just about wheat and water. Mostly, it's about time. Bread has a particular soul. Bread depends on time to be right. In both, it is baking and eating; bread leaves a mark on the consumer that acknowledges that every grain of bread is a life cycle away from its final, highest point. It needs time to be right and to become something more.

What is the highest point of bread? Can there be higher points than the thousand delicacies we proudly display and frame on our bookshelves, the daily new taste we all know so well? The answer is no. Because now, new recipes are coming to replace our old-world ways. In bread, even the greatest of recipes do not define the final product. They serve almost a form of parallelizing, both bread and human evolution. New recipes open doors across the world. Inspired by time, they allow our bread, once plentiful and yet to be discovered, to be found through time.

Now, let's get down to business. It is the bread machine cookbook. It is something that will inspire you to look further aside from the ordinary. It is something that'll make your kitchen a place that friends, family, and passersby will wonder, "how'd they do that?" The recipes here will do you right. They will save you money and give you more time between the old you and the new you.

So, what exactly is a bread machine? It is a device that works as a regular bread machine but allows you to experiment with different ingredients. If you are a beginner, it will serve as a tool for learning the correct way of making delicious bread. You will find that the methods of making particular delicious bread are not that hard. What's great is that, unlike a regular bread machine, the ingredients for the recipes in this cookbook do not have to be bought online but have to be found in the nearest grocery store. And, as a bonus for a limited time, you can get your first recipe at absolutely no charge here. With all that said, try some new bread recipes with your bread machine, and happy bread making!

CHAPTER 1:

Benefits and How to Use Bread Maker

Benefits of Bread Machine

While utilizing a bread machine for some may seem like a pointless advance, others don't envision existence without newly home-heated bread. In any case, how about we go to the realities – underneath, we indicated the advantages of owning a bread machine.

As a matter of first importance, you can appreciate the crisply prepared handcrafted bread. Most bread creators additionally include a clockwork, which permits you to set the preparing cycle at a specific time. This capacity is precious when you need to have moist bread toward the beginning of the day for breakfast.

You can control what you eat. By preparing bread at home, you can control what parts are coming into your portion. It is precious for individuals with sensitivities or for those who attempt to maintain the admission of a fixings' amount.

It is simple. A few people believe that preparing bread at home is chaotic, and by and large, it is a challenging procedure. In any case, preparing bread with a bread machine is a breeze. You pick the ideal choice and unwind - all the blending, rising, and heating process is going on within the bread producer, making it a zero-chaos process!

It saves you huge amounts of cash in the long haul. If you imagine that purchasing bread at a store is modest, you may be mixed up. It turns out that preparing bread at home will set aside your cash in the long haul, particularly if you have some dietary limitations.

Bread machines can make various kinds of bread; rye bread, sans gluten bread, whole wheat bread, and many more. They can also make pizza mixture, pasta batter, jam, and different heavenly dishes.

Incredible taste and quality, you have to acknowledge it – nothing beats the quality and taste of a crisp heap of bread. Since you are the person who is making bread, you can ensure that you utilize just the fixings that are new and of a high caliber. Homemade bread consistently beats locally acquired bread as far as taste and quality.

How to Use a Bread Machine

To begin with, you put the plying paddle inside the tin. When the tin is out of your bread machine, you can gauge the ingredients and put them into the prepared tin.

Later, you only need to put the pan inside your machine, pick the program you wish using the electronic board, and close the top. Here the bread producer enchantment dominates!

One of the main things the bread machine will do is working the batter – you will hear the sounds. On the off chance that your bread creator accompanies the preview window, you can watch the entire preparation procedure, which is very interesting.

After the massaging stage, everything will go calm for quite a while – the rising stage comes. The bread machine let the batter to rise. Then, there will be another set of controlling and demonstrating.

Finally, the bread maker broiler will on, and it will steam through the steam vent. Although the typical bread making process is programmed, most machines accompany formula books that give you various intriguing propelled bread plans.

The best thing about using a bread-making machine is it gets the hard cycle of bread making easy. You can use the bread-making machine in a full or complete cycle, especially for loaf bread, or you can do the dough cycle if you are baking bread that needs to bake in an oven. To use the bread-making machine, here are some steps to guide you:

Familiarize Yourself with The Parts and Button

Your bread-making machine has three essential parts, and without it, you will not be able to cook your bread. The first part is the machine itself, the second is the bread bucket, and the third is the kneading blade. The bread bucket and kneading blade are removable and replaceable. You can check with the manufacturer for parts to replace it if it's missing.

Learn how to operate your bread-making machine. Removing and placing the bread bucket back in is essential. Practice snapping the bread bucket on and off the machine until you are comfortable doing it. It is necessary because you don't want the bucket moving once the ingredients are in place.

Know Your Bread Bucket Capacity

It is an essential step before you start using the machine. If you load an incorrect measurement, you are going to have a big mess on your hand. To check your bread bucket capacity:

- Use a measuring cup for liquid and fill it with water.
- Pour the water on the bread bucket until it's full. Count how many cups of water you poured on the bread bucket.
- The number of cups of water will determine the size of your loaf of bread.

Less than 10 cups =1-pound loaf

10 cups =1 to 1 ½ pounds loaf

12 cups=1 or 1 ½ to 2 pounds loaf

14 cups or more=1 or ½ to 2 or 2 ½ pounds loaf

Learn the Basic Buttons and Settings

Here are some tips you can do to familiarize yourself with the machine:

- Read all the button labels. The buttons indicate the cycle in which your machine will mix, knead, and bake the bread.
- Basic buttons include start/stop, crust color, timer/arrow, select basic, sweet, whole wheat, French, gluten-free, quick/rapid, quick bread, jam, and dough.
- The Select setting or button allows you to choose the cycle you want in which you want to cook your loaf. It also includes a Dough cycle for oven-cooked bread.

Using the Delay Button

When you select a cycle, the machine sets a preset timer to bake the bread. For example, if you choose Basic, the time will be set by 3 hours. However, you want your bread cooked at a specific time, say, you want it in the afternoon, but it's only 7:00 in the morning. Your bread cooks for 3 hours, which means it will be done by 10:00 am, but you want it done by 12. You can use the arrow key for up and down to set the delay timer. Between 7 am and 12 noon, there is a difference of 5 hours, so you want your timer to be set at 5. Press the arrow keys up to add 2 hours to your timer so that your bread will cook in 5 hours instead of 3 hours. The delay button does not work if you are using the Dough cycle.

Order of Adding the Ingredients

This only matters if you are using the delay timer. It is essential to ensure that your yeast will not touch any liquid to activate it early. Early activation of the yeast could make your bread rise too much. If you plan to start the cycle immediately, you can add the ingredients in any order. However, adding the ingredients in order will discipline you to do it every time and make you less likely to forget it when necessary. To add the ingredients, do it in the following order:

- Place all the liquid fixings in the bread bucket.
- Add the sugar and the salt.
- Add the flour to cover and seal in the liquid ingredients.
- Add all the other remaining dry ingredients.
- Lastly, add the yeast. The yeast should not touch any liquid until the cooking cycle starts. When adding the yeast, make a small well using your finger to place the yeast to ensure yeast activation's proper timing.

Using the Dough Cycle

You cannot cook all bread using the bread-making machine, but you can use it to make the bread-making process easier. All bread goes under the dough cycle. If your bread needs to be oven-cooked, you can still use the bread-making machine by selecting the DOUGH cycle to mix and knead your flour into a dough. To start the Dough cycle:

- Add all your bread recipe ingredients to your bread bucket.
- Select the Dough cycle. It usually takes between 40 to 90 minutes.
- Press the Start button.
- After the cycle is complete, let your dough rest in the bread-making machine for 5 to 40 minutes.
- Take out the dough and start cutting into your desire shape.

Some machines have Pasta Dough or Cookie Dough cycle, which you can use for muffin recipes. However, if all you have is a basic dough setting, you can use it for the muffin recipe, but you need to stop the machine before the rising cycle begins.

CHAPTER 2:

Troubleshooting: Problem and Solution

The time has come to open up the bread machine finally, but low and behold, the bread that you have so hoped for resembles nothing of the sort. Flops and spills do happen from time to time. Here are a few answers to the questions you may have, depending on the appearance of your bread.

My Loaf Wasn't Cooked Inside.

If you bite into your bread and are left feeling like you are chewing on a piece of gum, then your thermostat could be faulty. If this frequently occurs, then look at your machine's thermostat since it's probably the problem. Using extra sugar or not measuring out your wet ingredients correctly can also cause this to happen.

My Loaf Didn't Rise or Only Rose Halfway.

So, your bread looks like a giant fluffed up the pancake and nothing like a loaf of bread? Old yeast, or forgotten yeast, will be your biggest culprit.

If too much salt was added, then you might be faced with a flat version of your bread, also, as the yeast won't be able to work appropriately (salt plays as an inhibitor to the yeast). The same issue might occur due to adding ingredients into the bread machine in the wrong order. Always follow the bread machine's instructions to prevent things like this from happening.

Specific flours also may contribute to this problem. Different flours will give different rises. Bread flour will provide you with a bigger loaf than all-purpose flour, while rye flour will provide you with a smaller loaf.

It Looks Like A Mushroom.

If your bread resembles a cloud that is left behind when a large bomb explodes, then you need to brush up on your measuring techniques. Often this is down to incorrect ingredient measurements.

Secondly, if you know deep down that you measured correctly, and followed the recipe step-by-step, then it could be due to your bread machine's pan size being too small for the job.

My Bread Is Far Too Dense.

For starters, dense bread could be down to having added too much or too little of something. It might happen if you add more nuts or dried fruit than needed. Adding more whole-grain flour than required will also affect the outcome of your bread.

If the recipe calls for only plain bread flour and you would like to incorporate whole-grain flour, consider using half of each rather than swapping one ingredient entirely.

There Are Big Holes in My Bread.

If your bread has holes too big and uneven, we suggest you can cast your gaze upon three culprits: yeast, salt, or water. Excess yeast can be the cause of extra air bubbles creating holes in the baked Loaf.

Or sometimes, if it is too warm in your kitchen, the yeast may have gotten more "oomph" than it needed causing the texture of your bread to change. In this case, and if you choose to make another loaf, use a pinch less yeast in your recipe.

If you skipped the salt, then holes may appear in your bread. Too much water can do the same for your bread. Adding nuts, fruits, or vegetables that have been rinsed or preserved in another liquid? Take a cloth and dry them off before adding them in.

My Bread Is Caved-In.

When opening the bread maker, you could be greeted by what looks like a prize-winning loaf of bread only to watch it cave in on itself. First things first, leave the machine to do its thing. Often, if you open and close the machine regularly while it is baking, this can cause your bread to collapse. The same might happen if you have not added salt or added too much yeast.

It is also essential to know what the capacity of your bread pan is. If your bread baking pan is too small for the job, then your bread may collapse.

My Bread Is Uneven.

If your bread is uneven or crooked, it could be that the bread machine's mixing paddles are not churning evenly or are out of rhythm with each other. Paddles can be worn out over time, so it is worth checking them if you have had your bread machine for some time. Alternatively, one of the paddles may have become wedged during the churning or kneading process.

My Bread Tastes Off.

The bread is perfect, just as you imagined it to be, but when you finally bite into it, it tastes weird or, frankly, tastes terrible. It is down to your ingredients and their freshness. Make sure you are storing your ingredients correctly and using the freshest ingredients possible.

CHAPTER 3:

How to Maintain Sourdough Starter

A sourdough starter is the "sour" in sourdough. It's a combination of flour, liquid, and yeast stored in a loosely covered jar or crock in the refrigerator. Frequent use or regular feeding keeps it alive. Some starters have been known to survive for generations!

There are probably as many sourdough starter recipes as there are wrinkles on an elephant. We won't go into them here; for now, we'd like to offer a few tips and facts for maintaining a sourdough starter.

Using A Starter

Bring refrigerated starter to room temperature before using it. You can place it in a bowl of warm water if you're in a hurry, or you can leave it out overnight if you plan to use it in the morning.

Like most things in life, the sourdough starter gets better with age. So don't be discouraged if your first bread doesn't quite live up to your sourest expectations. Just keep baking with it, and very soon, you'll notice it taking on its tangy personality.

Experiment. Use your sourdough starter in some of your favorite recipes. Rye bread is incredibly yummy when soured. If your starter is roughly half liquid and half flour, when you add starter to a recipe, consider half the starter amount used as liquid and reduce the liquid in the recipe by that amount. If you choose to add 1 cup sourdough starter to a rye bread recipe that lists 1¼ cups water, count the 1 cup starter as ½ cup liquid and deduct that amount from your 1¼ cups water. For that recipe, your liquids would be 1 cup sourdough starter and ¾ cup water.

Maintaining A Starter

After each use, the starter needs to be replenished with equal amounts of liquid and flour. Please do so, then cover it loosely and leave it out at room temperature for several hours until it increases and turns spongy-looking. Stir it down, then refrigerate.

Your starter should always be kept in the refrigerator or freezer. The exceptions, for those first few days as it's developing, the few hours before it's used, and the few hours after it's replenished or fed.

Feed your starter once a month if you are not using it. Add equal amounts of flour and warm liquid (90° to 100°F). Cover loosely and allow it to stand in a warm location (70° to 95°F) until it expands and turns spongy-looking. Stir it down and then place it in the refrigerator, loosely covered.

Remove the starter from its container every so often and give the container a good wash job in hot water.

Sourdough starter ages best when handled with tender, loving care. So, do remember to feed it. If you're going to be gone or know you won't be baking with your starter for an extended time, you can freeze it. When you choose to use it again, allow your starter to sit at room temperature for 24 hours to thaw out and return to life.

If you'd want to create a "backup" of your starter for safekeeping or share it with friends across the country, consider dehydrating some of it. Here's how:

Spoon enough starter on foam-type paper plates or large wax-paper—lined trays to coat the entire surface with a thin layer of starter. A thin coating will dry completely in approximately 24 hours. Once thoroughly dry, lift it off in large pieces and place it in a food processor, blender, or grain mill. Process briefly until coarsely ground.

Store and put in a glass jar or plastic bag someplace cool. When you are ready to rehydrate your dried starter, place ½ cup warm water (90° to 100°F) in a 1½-quart glass or ceramic container. Add ¼ cup ground starter and then ¼ cup flour. Stir well with a wooden spoon. Place the container in a warm location (between 75° and 95°F), and within several hours your starter should show signs of life with surface bubbles. At that point, add another ½ cup warm water and ½ cup more flour, stir, and allow the starter to feed overnight at room temperature before you use it or loosely cover it and store it in your refrigerator for later use.

If, after freezing or several weeks of nonuse, your starter looks a little sluggish and isn't displaying its usual bubbly personality, reserve 1 or 2 tablespoons of the starter in a separate bowl and pour the rest away. Thoroughly wash the container and place the reserved starter back into the clean container. Add 1 cup warm liquid (90° to 100°F) and 1 cup flour. Cover loosely and let it stand in a warm place (70° to 95°F) for several hours until bubbly and a clear liquid begins to form on top. You may be required to repeat it once or twice to bring it back to its bubbly, sour-smelling self again.

To maintain a 70° to 95°F temperature, place it in a warm location like an oven with a pilot light on, a warm kitchen, water heater's top, or refrigerator. During the day, put it in the sunshine, in a bowl filled with water set on a warming tray or directly on a heating pad.

CHAPTER 4:

Selecting the Right Kind of Yeast

Yeast is the biological leavening agent that is commonly used in bread to make it fluffier and softer. It is a fungus that ferments the dough to produce carbon dioxide and alcohol inside, and it raises the bread. Carbohydrates and sugar present inside the dough are broken and processed by the yeast, and in doing so, make the dough more stretchable and elastic. If you want to bake more often, yeast is the ingredient you must learn about well and study. How to deal with it takes some time and suitable conditions to work correctly. Many people complain their bread was not as fluffy and soft as they expected it to be; it is usually the leavening stage from where the problem starts.

The dough rises, but it does not look or taste like it should. The flour that you use is usually on the dry side, and when the dough is rolled out, the top surface will become dry and crack. Others have used too much yeast while the rest add pre-ferment sugar. The flour is too dry and doesn't hydrate the yeast properly, and it goes dormant. The yeast you buy is impure and probably too old. You must always check the expiry date before purchase yeast. Some people don't know how to handle the yeast properly, so they won't let the dough ferment as it should. The bread then becomes unfit for consumption.

One should pick up the right kind of yeast to bake bread and dough so that it would not fail because of the wrong one.

Kind of Yeast

Yeast comes in several forms and varieties in the market to use it according to the recipes. For bread-making, there are four types of yeast available that you should go for:

Active dry yeast

Instant yeast/quick-rising yeast

Fresh yeast

Bread machine yeast

Each type of yeast has a different working time, and they need slightly different conditions to work correctly.

Active Dry Yeast

This yeast comes in a dry form, and it needs to be activated. The activation can be carried out by hydrating the yeast. Small packets of active dry yeast are available; it takes a teaspoon of yeast to leaven the dough made with two flour cups. But before adding the yeast to the flour mixture, it is essential to mix it with the sugar and lukewarm water solution.

Leave this yeast mixer for about ten minutes at room temperature, and a light foam will appear on top of the mixture; this is the point where you add the other ingredients to make the dough. When it is ready, the bread is left for at least two hours for the yeast to work.

Instant Yeast/Quick-Rising Yeast

This yeast does not need any activation time; instead, it can be used directly. It comes in a fine granulated form, which is easily added to the dough like other ingredients. This yeast's quality is that it works to absorb the moisture into the bread and break down the sugar that is present in the dough. Once the yeast is mixed with the dough, it needs warmer temperatures to initiate leavening.

Fresh Yeast

Professionals often use fresh yeast, and it has the quickest working time. It is strong in flavor and aroma, and even a small amount can quickly raise the bread. Fresh yeast comes in compact moist squares, which are then dissolved in the water solution to mix with the other dough's other ingredients. This yeast infuses a powerful and distinct aroma in the bread, which can be noticed in bakery-baked bread.

CHAPTER 5:

White Bread

1. Amish Bread

It is a delicious recipe. It is adapted from an old Amish recipe but made in the bread machine.

Preparation time: 5 minutes

Cooking time: 3 hours

Servings: 12

Ingredients:

- 2 3/4 cups bread flour
- 1/4 cup canola oil
- 1 teaspoon active dry yeast
- 1/4 cup white sugar
- 1/2 teaspoon salt
- 18 tablespoons warm water

Directions:

1. Put the fixings in the pan of the bread machine in the order recommended by the manufacturer. Select White Bread cycle; press Start.
2. When the dough has raised once and the second cycle of kneading begins, turn the machine off. Reset by pressing Start once again before baking.

Nutrition:

Calories: 58 Fat: 4.7 g

Carbohydrate: 4.3 g Protein: 0.1 g

2. Apricot Oat Bread

Apricot oat bread is a tasty white bread for your bread machine.

Preparation time: 10 minutes

Cooking time: 30 minutes

Servings: 12

Ingredients: 4 1/4 cups bread flour

- 2/3 cup rolled oats
- 1 tablespoon white sugar
- 2 teaspoons active dry yeast

- 1 1/2 teaspoons salt
- 1 teaspoon ground cinnamon
- 2 tablespoons butter, cut up
- 1 2/3 cups orange juice
- 1/2 cup diced dried apricots
- 2 tablespoons honey, warmed

Directions:

1. Put the bread fixings in the pan of the bread machine in the order recommended by the manufacturer; add the dried apricots just before the kneading cycle ends.
2. Remove the bread promptly from the machine when it's finished, and glaze with the warmed honey. Allow cooling completely before serving.

Nutrition: Calories: 80 Fat: 2.3 g

Carbohydrate: 14.4 g Protein: 1.3 g

3. Basic White Bread

Nothing essential, just a basic white bread for your bread machine, though, sometimes the simple things in life are the best!

Preparation time: 5 minutes

Cooking time: 3 hours

Servings: 12

Ingredients: 1 1/4 cups warm water

- 1 tablespoon butter, softened
- 1 tablespoon white sugar
- 1 teaspoon salt
- 3 cups bread flour
- 2 tablespoons dry milk powder
- 1 (.25 ounce) package active dry yeast

Directions:

1. Put the fixings in the pan of the bread machine in the order recommended by the manufacturer. Select White Bread setting; press Start.

Nutrition: Calories: 142 Fat: 1.6 g

Carbohydrate: 26.7 g Protein: 4.8 g

4. Basil and Sundried Tomato Bread

This hearty, herb whited bread goes great with pasta!

Preparation time: 15 minutes

Cooking time: 3 hours

Servings: 12

Ingredients:

- 2 1/4 teaspoons active dry yeast

- 3 cups bread flour
- 3 tablespoons wheat bran
- 1/3 cup quinoa
- 3 tablespoons instant powdered milk
- 1 tablespoon dried basil
- 1/3 cup chopped sun-dried tomatoes
- 1 teaspoon salt
- 1 1/4 cups water
- 1 cup boiling water to cover

Directions:

1. Put the boiling water over sun-dried tomato halves to cover in a small bowl. Soak within 10 minutes, drain, then cool to room temperature. With scissors, snip into 1/4-inch pieces.
2. Put all the fixings into the pan of the bread machine in the order recommended by the manufacturer. Select the Basic or White Bread cycle, and Start.

Nutrition:

Calories: 156 Fat: 1 g

Carbohydrate: 30.6 g Protein: 5.9 g

5. Baxi's White Bread

A very simple but hearty white bread for the bread machine.

Preparation time: 5 minutes

Cooking time: 2 hours & 15 minutes

Servings: 10

Ingredients:

- 1 1/2 teaspoons active dry yeast
- 2 cups bread flour
- 1 teaspoon salt
- 1 tablespoon white sugar
- 1 tablespoon dry milk powder
- 1 tablespoon butter, softened
- 3/4 cup water

Directions:

1. Put the fixings in the pan of the bread machine in the order recommended by the manufacturer. Select Medium cycle; press Start. When done, remove bread from pan and let cool on a wire rack.

Nutrition:

Calories: 19

Fat: 1.2 g

Carbohydrate: 1.9 g

Protein: 0.5 g

6. Best Bread Machine Bread

It is a bread read recipe that is easy and foolproof. This bread is soft and tasty with a flaky crust.

Preparation time: 10 minutes

Cooking time: 40 minutes

Servings: 12

Ingredients:

- 1 cup warm water at 110 F
- 2 tbsp white sugar
- 1 package bread machine yeast
- 1/4 cup vegetable oil
- 3 cups bread flour
- 1 teaspoon salt

Directions:

1. Put the water, sugar, plus yeast in the pan of your bread machine. Allow the yeast to melt and foam within 10 minutes. Put the oil, flour, plus salt into it. Choose Basic/White Bread, then click Start.

Nutrition:

Calories: 174 Fat: 5.2 g

Carbohydrate: 27.1 g Protein: 4.3 g

7. Buttermilk White Bread

It is a great white bread recipe; dried buttermilk powder allows using your bread machine's delayed timer feature. Wake up to fresh bread!

Preparation time: 5 minutes

Cooking time: 3 hours

Servings: 12

Ingredients:

- 1 1/8 cups water
- 3 tablespoons honey
- 1 tablespoon margarine
- 1 1/2 teaspoons salt
- 3 cups bread flour
- 2 teaspoons active dry yeast
- 4 tablespoons powdered buttermilk

Directions:

1. Put the fixings to your machine pan. Click medium crust, then White bread. Then, press start.

Nutrition:

Calories: 34 Fat: 1 g Carbohydrate: 5.7 g

Protein: 1 g

8. Cinnamon Swirl Bread

This bread is probably the best thing you will make in your bread maker.

Preparation time: 1 hour & 15 minutes

Cooking time: 30 minutes

Servings: 24

Ingredients:

- 1 cup milk
- 2 eggs
- 1/4 cup butter
- 4 cups bread flour
- 1/4 cup white sugar
- 1 teaspoon salt
- 1 1/2 teaspoons active dry yeast
- 1/2 cup chopped walnuts
- 1/2 cup packed brown sugar
- 2 teaspoons ground cinnamon
- 2 tablespoons softened butter, divided
- 2 teaspoons sifted confectioners' sugar, divided (optional)

Directions:

1. Put the milk, eggs, 1/4 cup butter, bread flour, sugar, salt, yeast into your machine, choose the dough setting and start.
2. Move the dough to a floured work empty surface, then punch down. Let dough rest for 10 minutes. Mix the walnuts, brown sugar, plus cinnamon in a bowl.
3. Split dough in half, then rolls each half into a rectangle about 9x14 inches. Spread 1 tablespoon softened butter over each dough rectangle, then sprinkle dough with half the walnut batter. Roll dough rectangles from the short ends, then pinch it closed.
4. Oiled 2 9x5-inch loaf pans, then put the rolled loaves into it with seam sides down. Cover, then let rise within 30 minutes.
5. Warm your oven to 350 F. Bake loaves in the preheated oven until lightly golden brown and bread sounds hollow when tapped, about 30 minutes.
6. If loaves brown too quickly, lightly cover with aluminum foil for the last 10 minutes of baking. Let the bread cool within 10 minutes before removing to finish cooling on wire racks. Sprinkle over with 1 teaspoon confectioners' sugar.

Nutrition:

Calories: 80

Fat: 5.1 g

Carbohydrate: 7.9 g

Protein: 1.4 g

9. Cottage Cheese Bread

It is a hearty white bread that you will put in your bread machine, and the kids will love it.

Preparation time: 5 minutes

Cooking time: 3 hours

Servings: 12

Ingredients:

- 1/2 cup water
- 1 cup cottage cheese
- 2 tablespoons margarine
- 1 egg
- 1 tablespoon white sugar
- 1/4 teaspoon baking soda
- 1 teaspoon salt
- 3 cups bread flour
- 2 1/2 teaspoons active dry yeast

Directions:

1. Put the fixings to your machine, and start. You can use up to 1/2 cup more bread flour if the dough seems too sticky.

Nutrition: Calories: 171 Fat: 3.6 g

Carbohydrate: 26.8 g Protein: 7.3 g

10. Yeasted Cornbread

This bread develops a lovely, fragrant layer of yeast on top. Like any yeast bread, you'll know it's done if the surface is covered with little air bubbles. Because it's dense and moist, this bread stays fresh for a long time.

Preparation time: 5 minutes

Cooking time: 3 hours

Servings: 12

Ingredients: 3 1/2 cups bread flour

- 1/2 cup cornmeal
- 1 teaspoon salt
- 3 tablespoons white sugar
- 3 tablespoons shortening
- 1 cup milk - 1/8 cup water
- 1 egg
- 2 1/2 teaspoons active dry yeast

Directions:

1. Put the fixings in the bread machine pan in the order suggested by the manufacturer. Select the Basic or White Bread setting, and start the machine. Transfer the bread from the pan to a rack to cool. Wrap in foil to store.

Nutrition: Calories: 77 Fat: 4.2 g

Carbohydrate: 8.3 gProtein: 1.9 g

11. Homemade Wonderful Bread

It is a white bread without a strong yeast flavor.

Preparation time: 10 minutes

Cooking time: 3 hours

Servings: 15

Ingredients:

- 2 1/2 teaspoons active dry yeast
- 1/4 cup warm water (110 degrees F/45 degrees C)
- 1 tablespoon white sugar
- 4 cups all-purpose flour
- 1/4 cup dry potato flakes
- 1/4 cup dry milk powder
- 2 teaspoons salt
- 1/4 cup white sugar
- 2 tablespoons margarine
- 1 cup warm water at 110 F

Directions:

1. Whisk together the yeast, 1/4 cup warm water, and sugar. Allow sitting for 15 minutes. Put the fixings in the order suggested by your manufacturer, including the yeast mixture. Select the basic and light crust setting.

Nutrition:

Calories: 162

Fat: 1.8 g

Carbohydrate: 31.6 g

Protein: 4.5 g

12. Honey White Bread

Honey White bread is a simple recipe with a soft and tender interior; eaten with butter, jam, or cheese, it makes the perfect blend of sweetness and consistency in many dishes.

Preparation time: 15 minutes

Cooking time: 3 hours

Servings: 12

Ingredients:

- 1 cup milk
- 3 tbsp unsalted butter, melted
- 2 tbsp honey
- 3 cups bread flour
- 3/4 tsp salt
- 3/4 tsp vitamin c powder
- 3/4 tsp ground ginger
- 1 1/2 tsp active dry yeast

Directions:

1. Put all the listed fixings in the order suggested in your bread machine manual. Select the Basic Bread cycle. Press starts.

Nutrition:

Calories: 172 Fat: 3.9 g

Carbohydrate: 28.9 g Protein: 5 g

13. Jos Rosemary Bread

It is a bread that has a great flavor. It is moist and has a crispy crust.

Preparation time: 10 minutes

Cooking time: 40 minutes

Servings: 12

Ingredients:

- 1 cup of water
- 3 tablespoons olive oil
- 1 1/2 teaspoons white sugar
- 1 1/2 teaspoons salt
- 1/4 teaspoon Italian seasoning
- 1/4 teaspoon ground black pepper
- 1 tablespoon dried rosemary
- 2 1/2 cups bread flour
- 1 1/2 teaspoons active dry yeast

Directions:

1. Put all the fixings in the pan of the bread machine in the order recommended by the manufacturer. Select white bread cycle; press Start.

Nutrition:

Calories: 137 Fat: 3.9 g

Carbohydrate: 21.6 g Protein: 3.6 g

14. Light Oat Bread

This bread is made with light, fluffy oats, fresh, summery scents, and flavors. The recipe is written to be used with a bread machine. The whole house will smell delightful while it is baking in the oven.

Preparation time: 5 minutes

Cooking time: 3 hours

Servings: 12

Ingredients:

- 1 1/4 cups water
- 2 tablespoons margarine
- 1 teaspoon salt
- 3 cups all-purpose flour

- 1/2 cup rolled oats
- 2 tablespoons brown sugar
- 1 1/2 teaspoons active dry yeast

Directions:

1. Put all the listed fixings above in the bread machine pan in order. Use regular light setting.

Nutrition:

Calories: 152 Fat: 2.3 g

Carbohydrate: 28.6 g Protein: 3.9 g

15. Alligator Animal Italian Bread

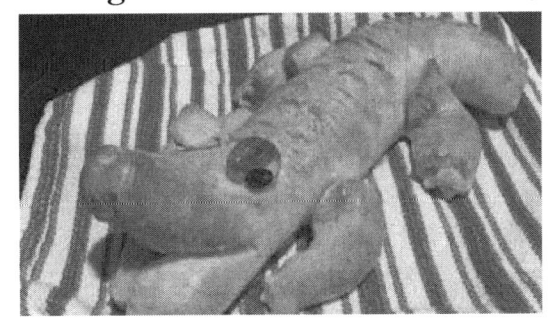

It is a simple Italian bread alligator-shaped.

Preparation time: 30 minutes

Cooking time: 2 hours

Servings: 8

Ingredients:

For the dough:

- 1 cup of warm water at 110 F
- 3 cups of all-purpose flour
- 1 tbsp vital wheat gluten (optional)
- 1 1/2 tsp salt
- 2 1/2 tsp instant yeast

For decorating:

- 2 raisins
- 1 egg
- 1 tsp water

Directions:

1. Mix the water, flour, gluten (optional), salt, plus yeast in your machine using the Dough cycle.
2. When the first rising completes, punch the dough down and move it to a lightly floured surface—oiled a baking sheet using parchment paper.
3. Roll out your dough into a square about 3/4-inch thick and split it into 4 pieces. Roll up 3 of them in jelly-roll style, then put them seam-side down on your baking sheet to shape the head, body, plus tail.
4. Oiled your hands, then shape your dough, elongate the tail to a slender curved tip, then slightly in the nose end.
5. Cut into the nose horizontally at the tip to form the mouth; hold the mouth open with a wedge of greased aluminum foil.
6. From the remaining quarter of the dough, cut off a tiny part for the eyes. Cut the rest into 4 logs for legs, flat one end of the legs, then insert it under the body.
7. Form the legs into slight bends when putting them on your baking sheet—slice short parts into the other end of the leg for the claws.
8. Snip shallow cuts over the dough surface using scissors. Roll the reserved dough into mini balls for the eyes, stuff each using a raisin.

9. Warm oven to 400 F, then mix the egg and 1 tbsp of warm water in a small bowl.
10. Allow the alligator dough to rise in a warm place within 30minutes. Slightly brush the dough with the egg wash and bake it in the preheated oven until golden brown, about 20 minutes.
11. Remove the alligator from the baking sheet with a spatula and transfer it to a wire rack. Remove the aluminum foil when cool.

Nutrition:

Calories: 187

Fat: 1.1 g

Carbohydrate: 36.7 g

Protein: 6.6 g

CHAPTER 6:

Wholegrain Bread

16. Seven-Grain Bread

This bread is lovely. It has a great, soft texture but has a nice brown crust. Because it is retarded, it makes a dense loaf, not a crumbly one.

Preparation time: 10 minutes

Cooking time: 3 hours

Servings: 1 loaf

Ingredients:

- 2 1/4 tsp dry yeast
- 1 1/2 cups whole wheat flour
- 1 cup of bread flour
- 1 tsp salt
- 1/2 cup crumbled 7-grain cereal flakes
- 3 tbsp nonfat dry milk
- 1 tbsp unsweetened cocoa powder
- 2 tbsp butter or margarine
- 1/8 cup dark molasses
- 1 cup warm water at 100 to 105 degrees
- 3 tablespoons warm water

Directions:

1. Add all ingredients to the machine in the order recommended by machine manufacturers. Select "Whole Wheat" bread setting; crust color light.

Nutrition: Calories: 190 Carbs: 38g

Fat: 3g Protein: 6g

17. Seven-Grain Oat Molasses Bread

7-Grain Oat Molasses Bread is a much healthier version of grain bread. You can add raisins or dried fruit if you like and a few more or different grains and nuts. It is delicious alone or toasted and buttered.

Preparation time: 2 hours

Cooking time: 1 hour & 35 minutes

Servings: 11

Ingredients:

- 1 1/3 cups warm water (faucet warm)
- 1 teaspoon Extra virgin olive oil
- 2+ teaspoons Honey
- 1/3+ cup Molasses
- 1 cup Whole Grain Rolled Oats - uncooked
- 2 cups unbleached white flour
- 1 cup whole wheat flour
- 1/2 cup buckwheat flour
- 1/4 cup flax seed
- 1/4 cup chia seeds
- 1/4 cup sunflower seeds
- 1/4 cup pecans
- 3 teaspoons active dry yeast

Directions:

1. Put the listed fixings in the pan of your bread machine in the order ingredients are listed. Select wheat bread setting, large loaf, and Start. Slice into 11 pieces.

Nutrition:

Calories: 183

Carbs: 37g

Fat: 0g

Protein: 4g

18. Eight-Grain Bread

This bread is a good one to use for toast and sandwiches. It is a very moist, heavy bread.

Preparation time: 10 minutes

Cooking time: 1 and 30 minutes to 2 hours

Servings: 1 loaf

Ingredients:

- 1 package active dry yeast
- 1 1/2 cups bread flour
- 1 1/2 cups 8-grain flour
- 1 tablespoon sugar
- 1/8 cup corn oil
- 1 teaspoon salt
- 3/4 cup warm milk
- 1/4 cup warm water

Directions:

1. Put all the fixings on the machine in order. Select "whole wheat" bread setting; then crust color light.

Nutrition:

Calories: 160 Carbs: 30g

Fat: 2g Protein: 6g

19. Ten Grain Bread

Ten Grain Bread is a moist bread recipe using a Bread Machine; this bread recipe makes a large loaf that bakes up beautifully.

Preparation time: 20 minutes

Cooking time: 2 hours

Servings: 13

Ingredients:

- 1 package 10 Grain Bread Mix
- 3 teaspoons Canola Oil (or other oil)
- 1-1/4 cups water - warm

Directions:

1. For a 1-1/2-pound bread machine, put warm tap water into the machine. Locate and remove the enclosed yeast packet.
2. Then add the contents of the package of the 10 Grain Bread Mix, oil, and contents of the yeast packet.
3. Set machine to basic white bread or medium setting. Turn the device on. Now, enjoy the best whole grain bread you've ever made.

Nutrition:

Calories: 80 Carbs: 16g

Fat: 1g Protein: 5g

20. Bread Machine Multigrain Loaf

This bread machine recipe makes a nutritious and delicious multigrain loaf.

Preparation time: 10 minutes

Cooking time: 3 hours & 30 minutes

Servings: 12

Ingredients:

- 1 1/4 cups water
- 2 tablespoons butter or margarine, softened
- 1 1/3 cups bread flour
- 1 1/3 cups whole wheat flour
- 1 cup 7-grain or hot multigrain cereal (uncooked)
- 3 tablespoons packed brown sugar
- 1 1/4 teaspoons salt
- 2 1/2 teaspoons bread machine yeast

Directions:

1. Put all the fixings in the machine pan. Click Basic/White cycle, then Medium/Light crust color. Remove baked bread from pan; cool on a cooling rack.

Nutrition: Calories 170g Fat 2.5 g

Carbohydrate 31g Protein 5g

21. Whole-Grain Sesame Bread

Whole-Grain Sesame Bread is full of vitamin, mineral, and dietary fiber. The taste is delicious. The crust of the bread is crispy.

Preparation time: 5 minutes

Cooking time: 25 minutes

Servings: 20

Ingredients:

- 1 1/4 cups buttermilk
- 2 tbsp butter
- 1 tbsp sugar
- 1/4 cup honey
- 1/4 cup sesame seeds
- 2 tbsp wheat germ
- 2 tbsp nonfat dry milk powder
- 1 1/2 tsp salt
- 2 1/4 cups bread flour
- 1 cup whole wheat flour
- 3/4 cup rye flour
- 3 1/2 tsp bread machine yeast

Directions:

1. Put the fixings in the bread machine, then set to Whole Wheat. Check the dough after 5 minutes. The dough should be smooth and slightly sticky to the touch.
2. You may also remove the dough after kneading and bake in the oven at 350F until well browned, about 25 minutes.

Nutrition:

Calories 134.4 Fat 2.6 g

Carbohydrate 24.4 g Protein 4.2 g

22. Spent Grain Wheat Bread

This bread is great to use some of the grain leftovers when brewing beer. Just make sure that you aren't using spent grain that has hops mixed in with it.

Preparation time: 15 minutes

Cooking time: 40 minutes

Servings: 12

Ingredients:

- 1 1/4 cups water
- 3 tablespoons honey
- 3 tablespoons butter, softened
- 1/4 cup spent grain
- 1 1/2 tablespoons powdered milk
- 1 teaspoon white sugar
- 1 teaspoon salt

- 1/2 cup rye flour
- 1 1/2 cups whole wheat flour
- 1 1/2 cups bread flour
- 1/4 cup vital wheat gluten
- 1 teaspoon active dry yeast

Directions:

1. Put the listed fixings in the pan of the machine. Select whole wheat cycle; press Start. If using the delay timer, decrease water by 1 tablespoon.

Nutrition: Calories: 189 Carbs: 37g

Fat: 2g Protein: 5g

23. Seven-Grain Millet Bread

This Seven-Grain Millet Bread is dense, moist, and flavorful. The combination of the ingredients produces a satisfying taste.

Preparation time: 2 hours

Cooking time: 40 minutes

Servings: 1 loaf

Ingredients:

- 2 1/4 teaspoons yeast
- 2 1/3 cups bread flour
- 2/3 cup seven-grain flour
- 1/3 cup millet seeds - lightly toasted
- 1 1/2 teaspoons salt
- 4 tablespoons powdered milk
- 1 tablespoon butter or margarine
- 3/4 cup water - 3 tablespoons honey
- 1 large egg
- 1 teaspoon lemon juice

Directions:

1. Put all the listed fixings in the bread machine and push Start!

Nutrition Calories: 207 Carbs: 41g

Fat: 2g Protein: 6g

24. Seven Grain Bread II

This bread is perfect with a pot of bean soup or a slice of cold, fresh goat cheese on a hot day.

Preparation time: 10 minutes

Cooking time: 1 hour & 30 minutes

Servings: 10

Ingredients:

- 1 1/3 cups warm water at 110 degrees F

- 1 tablespoon active dry yeast
- 3 tablespoons dry milk powder
- 2 tablespoons vegetable oil
- 2 tablespoons honey
- 2 teaspoons salt
- 1 egg
- 1 cup whole wheat flour
- 2 1/2 cups bread flour
- 3/4 cup
- 7-grain cereal

Directions:

1. Put all listed fixings in the bread machine pan in the order suggested by the manufacturer. Select Whole Wheat Bread cycle, and Start.

Nutrition:

Calories: 150

Carbs: 26g

Fat: 25g

Protein: 1g

25. Multigrain Raisin Bread

If you haven't already tried the great, nutty taste of multigrain bread, then whip up a batch of this recipe today.

Preparation time: 5 minutes

Cooking time: 3 hours

Servings: 1 loaf

Ingredients:

- 1 cup of water
- 1 tablespoon butter
- 2 tablespoon honey
- 1 cup White Flour
- 1 cup Multigrain Blend
- 1 teaspoon salt
- 3/4 teaspoon cinnamon
- 3/4 teaspoon bread machine yeast
- 1/2 cup raisins

Directions:

1. Choose a loaf size, then put all listed fixings above on your machine. Select White/Whole Wheat, then start.

Nutrition:

Calories 353

Protein 10.1 g

Fat 4.2 g

Carbohydrate 71.9 g

CHAPTER 7:

Rye Bread

26. Basic Rye Bread

It is a simple rye bread prepared in the bread machine. For a better rise, more sugar is added.

Preparation time: 5 minutes

Cooking time: 3 hours

Servings: 12

Ingredients:

- 1 1/8 cups warm water
- 2 tbsps. Molasses
- 1 tbsp. vegetable oil - 1 tsp. salt
- 2 cups all-purpose flour
- 1 1/2 cups rye flour
- 3 tbsps. packed brown sugar
- 1 tbsp. unsweetened cocoa powder
- 3/4 tsp. caraway seed
- 2 tsp. bread machine yeast

Directions:

1. Assemble the ingredients as directed by your bread machine's manufacturer. Then select the settings for whole wheat and light crust.

Nutrition: Calories: 159 Carbohydrate: 32.5 g

Fat: 1.6 g Protein: 3.6 g

27. Buttermilk Rye Bread

Buttermilk Rye Bread is lovely, and it makes beautiful toast, is fantastic in sandwiches, and is beautiful for an open face with turkey, chicken, and melted cheese.

Preparation time: 45 minutes

Cooking time: 1 hour & 15 minutes

Servings: 15

Ingredients:

- 1 1/3 cups water

- 2 tbsps. vegetable oil
- 2 tbsps. honey
- 1 1/2 tbsps. vinegar
- 2 tbsps. powdered buttermilk
- 2 1/3 cups bread flour
- 1 cup rye flour
- 1/3 cup dry potato flakes
- 1 tsp. salt
- 2 tsp. active dry yeast
- 1 tsp. caraway seed

Directions:

1. Add the ingredients following the order given by the machine's manufacturer into the bread machine pan. Then set the machine to the setting for Basic or White Bread and push the start button.

Nutrition:

Calories: 59

Carbohydrate: 9.3 g

Fat: 2 g

Protein: 1.2 g

28. Caraway Rye Bread

This light rye loaf is nicely flavored and has lots of caraway seeds. It's sweetened with molasses and brown sugar. Let to cool before cutting.

Preparation time: 10 minutes

Cooking time: 4 hours & 10 minutes

Servings: 12

Ingredients:

- 1 1/4 cups lukewarm water (100 degrees F/38 degrees C)
- 2 tbsps. dry milk powder
- 1 tsp. salt
- 2 tbsps. brown sugar
- 2 tbsps. molasses
- 2 tbsps. butter
- 3/4 cup whole wheat flour
- 1 3/4 cups bread flour
- 3/4 cup rye flour
- 1 1/2 tbsps. caraway seeds
- 1 3/4 tsp. active dry yeast

Directions:

1. In the bread machine pan, add water at room temperature, milk powder, salt, brown sugar, molasses, butter, whole wheat flour, bread flour, rye flour, caraway seeds, and yeast. Use the setting for the Grain and 2-lb loaf size.

Nutrition:

Calories: 93

Carbohydrate: 16.5 g

Fat: 2.3 g

Protein: 2.4 g

29. Chai Cake

It isn't exactly a coffee cake but rather a bread machine cake that is very moist. This bread turned out to be great in the morning or as a snack/dessert. You can top your slices with strawberry cream cheese, although you can top with anything to satisfy your sweet tooth. Preparation time: 15 minutes

Cooking time: 3 hours & 55 minutes

Servings: 10

Ingredients:

- 1 (1.1 oz) package chai tea powder
- 3/4 cup hot water
- 1/4 cup Chardonnay wine
- 1/2 tsp. vanilla extract - 1 egg yolk
- 1/2 cup frozen unsweetened raspberries - 1/4 cup rye flour
- 1 tbsp. butter, room temperature
- 1/2 cup bread flour
- 1 cup all-purpose flour
- 1/2 cup wheat bran
- 1 (.25 oz.) package active dry yeast
- 1/2 cup coarsely chopped walnuts
- 1/2 tsp. caraway seed
- 1/4 cup white sugar
- 1 tsp. coarse smoked salt flakes

Directions:

1. Use 1 packet or 2 tbsp of dry mix mixed into 3/4 cup of hot water to make the chai tea. Let to cool for around ten 10 minutes.
2. Into bread machine pan, mix the chai tea, Chardonnay, vanilla extract, egg yolk, frozen raspberries, and butter. Then pour in bread flour, rye flour, all-purpose flour, wheat bran, yeast, walnuts, caraway seed, sugar, and salt.
3. Set machine to "Sweet" setting with a "Light Crust" and press the start button. Once bread finishes baking, let it cool for a minimum of half an hour before slicing. Serve.

Nutrition:

Calories: 184 Carbohydrate: 27.9 g

Fat: 6.3 g Protein: 4.3 g

30. Danish Rugbrod

Danish Rugbrod bread is made from a very spongy dough. The rye gives it a unique texture and the butter an impressive bite.

Preparation time: 10 minutes

Cooking time: 3 hours & 10 minutes

Servings: 24

Ingredients:

- 1 1/2 cups water
- 1 tbsp. honey
- 1 tbsp. butter

- 1 tsp. salt
- 2 cups rye flour
- 1 cup all-purpose flour
- 1 cup whole wheat flour
- 1/4 cup rye flakes (optional)
- 1 tbsp. white sugar
- 2 tsp. bread machine yeast

Directions:

1. Into the bread machine pan, add the following in this order: water, honey, butter, salt, rye flour, all-purpose flour, whole wheat flour, rye flakes, sugar, and yeast. Set the machine to the setting for basic and start it.

Nutrition:

Calories: 80

Carbohydrate: 16.5 g

Fat: 0.8 g

Protein: 2.2 g

31. Danish Spiced Rye Bread

An old-fashioned Danish rye bread that is made easy by using the bread machine. This highly spiced bread is excellent with Danish open-faced sandwiches (smorebrod) and mostly served on a Christmas holiday. It's perfect for individuals who love a spiced twist to their bread.

Preparation time: 20 minutes

Cooking time: 3 hours & 25 minutes

Servings: 16

Ingredients:

- 1 cup milk
- 1 cup of water
- 3 tbsps. butter
- 1/2 cup light molasses
- 1/3 cup white sugar
- 1 tbsp. grated orange zest
- 1 tbsp. fennel seed
- 1 tbsp. anise seed
- 1 tbsp. caraway seed
- 1 tbsp. cardamom
- 1 tsp. salt
- 2 (.25 oz.) packages active dry yeast
- 1/4 cup warm water at 110 F
- 2 cups rye flour
- 5 cups all-purpose flour
- 3 tbsps. butter, melted

Directions:

1. Warm milk in a medium saucepan until it's scalding and small bubbles form around the edges, and just before the milk starts to boil.
2. Remove the pan from the heat source and mix in the caraway seed, water, orange zest, butter, salt, molasses, cardamom, sugar, and anise seed. Let to step and cool for half an hour at lukewarm.
3. Mix the warm water and the yeast in a bread maker and then leave to stand for 5 minutes. Add the spice

mixture and cooled milk into the bread machine containing the yeast mixture.
4. Pour the flour into the bread machine. Set to dough cycle and then run it. Coat two 9x5 inch loaf pans with grease.
5. Once the dough cycle is done, take out the dough from the machine, separate it in half, shape into two loaves, and then transfer to the loaf pans prepared.
6. Cover loaves and rise within 30 minutes or until a small dent is formed on the loaves when you poke with your finger.
7. Warm oven to 375 F, then bake within 35 to 40 minutes until the loaves sound hollow once tapped at the bottom. Use melted butter to rub the hot loaves and then let to cool before serving.

Nutrition:

Calories: 287 Carbohydrate: 53.5 g

Fat: 5.5 g Protein: 6.4 g

32. Health Dynamics Rye Bread

The use of rye flour is evident in the crackling crisp crumb, the pleasant mild sour tang, and the unyielding firmness. It is bread for people who like to put their teeth into a long, chewy mouthful.

Preparation time: 15 minutes

Cooking time: 46 minutes

Servings: 12

Ingredients:

- 2 eggs
- 3/4 cup warm water
- 2 tbsps. vegetable oil
- 2 tbsps. molasses
- 2 1/2 cups rye flour
- 1/4 cup cornstarch
- 2 tsp. lecithin
- 1 1/4 tsp. sea salt
- 3 tsp. active dry yeast

Directions:

1. Into the bread machine pan, put the ingredients in the order suggested by the manufacturer. Set the machine to the setting for Regular cycle and medium crust and push Start.
2. Check the consistency of the dough as it mixes. It should be a little bit sticky.

Nutrition:

Calories: 136

Carbohydrate: 21.8 g

Fat: 4.3 g

Protein: 3.4 g

33. Montana Russian Black Bread

It is a very flavorful and healthy bread, and a little goes a long way. You'll want to serve it with lots of butter!

Preparation time: 20 minutes

Cooking time: 3 hours & 35 minutes

Servings: 10

Ingredients:

- 2 1/2 cups whole wheat bread flour
- 1 cup rye flour
- 3 tbsps. unsweetened cocoa powder
- 2 tbsps. bread flour
- 1 tbsp. wheat germ
- 1 tbsp. caraway seeds
- 2 tsp. active dry yeast
- 1 cup flat warm porter beer
- 1/2 cup strong brewed coffee
- 2 tbsps. balsamic vinegar
- 2 tbsps. olive oil
- 2 tbsps. honey
- 1 tbsp. molasses
- 1 tsp. sea salt
- 1/4 tsp. onion powder
- 1 egg white
- 1 tbsp. warm water

Directions:

1. In the bread machine, put in the whole wheat bread flour, rye flour, cocoa powder, bread flour, wheat germ, caraway seeds, yeast, beer, coffee, vinegar, olive oil, honey, molasses, sea salt, and onion powder, following the order of ingredients recommended by the manufacturer.
2. Choose the kneading cycle on the machine. Using your parchment paper to line the bottom of a baking sheet.
3. Take the dough out from the bread machine, place it onto the prepared baking sheet, form the dough into the shape of a rustic loaf.
4. Cut slits in a crisscross pattern on the top surface of the loaf. Allow the dough to rise in volume for 1 hour— Preheat the oven to 395°F (202°C).
5. In a small bowl, combine the warm water and egg white. Use a brush to coat the top of the loaf with the egg white mixture.
6. Put in the preheated oven and bake for 45-50 minutes until the bread is thoroughly cooked. Cool down for 1 hour before serving.

Nutrition:

Calories: 241

Carbohydrate: 41.4 g

Fat: 4.5 g

Protein: 8.3 g

34. Mustard Wheat Rye Sandwich Bread

This sandwich bread is fantastic. It makes the perfect Rueben sandwich or grilled cheese! You can shape the bread in a circle and then bake free form in la cloche.

Preparation time: 5 minutes

Cooking time: 3 hours & 5 minutes

Servings: 12

Ingredients:

- 1 cup warm water at 110 F
- 1/2 cup Dijon-style prepared mustard
- 2 tbsps. olive oil
- 1 1/2 tbsps. molasses
- 2 cups unbleached all-purpose flour
- 2/3 cup rye flour
- 2/3 cup whole wheat flour
- 1 1/2 tbsps. vital wheat gluten
- 2 1/2 tsp. active dry yeast

Directions:

1. Into the bread machine pan, assemble all the ingredients according to the machine maker's instructions. Then use the setting for basic or white bread and press start.

Nutrition:

Calories: 163

Carbohydrate: 29.9 g

Fat: 2.7 g

Protein: 4.5 g

35. New York Rye Bread

This bread has an intense rye flavor; it's traditionally baked in a bread machine. It's good with corned beef, pastrami, or sauerkraut.

Preparation time: 5 minutes

Cooking time: 3 hours & 5 minutes

Servings: 12

Ingredients:

- 1 1/8 cups warm water
- 1 1/3 tbsps. vegetable oil
- 2 tbsps. honey
- 1 tsp. salt
- 2 2/3 tsp. caraway seed
- 1 1/3 cups rye flour

- 2 1/3 cups bread flour
- 1/4 cup vital wheat gluten
- 1/4 cup dry milk powder
- 2 1/2 tsp. active dry yeast

Directions:

1. Put all the ingredients as directed by your machine's manual into the bread machine. Select the setting for cycle to Basic or White.

Nutrition:

Calories: 90

Carbohydrate: 14.8 g

Fat: 1.8 g

Protein: 3.9 g

CHAPTER 8:

Vegetable Breads

36. Healthy Celery Loaf

Healthy Celery Loaf is an easy recipe for kids cooking, which you can make at home. This celery loaf tastes very simple.

Preparation Time: 2 hours 40 minutes

Cooking time: 50 minutes

Servings: 1 loaf

Ingredients:

- 1 can (10 ounces) cream of celery soup
- 3 tablespoons low-fat milk, heated
- 1 tablespoon vegetable oil
- 1¼ teaspoons celery salt
- ¾ cup celery, fresh/sliced thin
- 1 tablespoon celery leaves, fresh, chopped
- 1 whole egg
- ¼ teaspoon sugar
- 3 cups bread flour
- ¼ teaspoon ginger
- ½ cup quick-cooking oats
- 2 tablespoons gluten
- 2 teaspoons celery seeds
- 1 pack of active dry yeast

Directions:

1. Put all of the fixings into your bread machine, carefully following the instructions of the manufacturer.
2. Set the program of your bread machine to Basic/White Bread and set crust type to Medium. Press starts.
3. Wait until the cycle completes. Once the loaf is ready, take the bucket out and let the loaf cool within 5 minutes. Shake the bucket to remove the loaf. Transfer, slice, and serve.

Nutrition:

Calories: 73

Fat: 4 g

Carbohydrates: 8 g

Protein: 3 g

37. Broccoli and Cauliflower Bread

Broccoli and Cauliflower Bread is for those of you who have a bread machine and want a bread recipe that is tasty and healthy.

Preparation Time: 2 hours 20 minutes

Cooking time: 50 minutes

Servings: 1 loaf

Ingredients:

- ¼ cup of water
- 4 tablespoons olive oil
- 1 egg white
- 1 teaspoon lemon juice
- 2/3 cup grated cheddar cheese
- 3 tablespoons green onion
- ½ cup broccoli, chopped
- ½ cup cauliflower, chopped
- ½ teaspoon lemon pepper seasoning
- 2 cups bread flour
- 1 teaspoon bread machine yeast

Directions:

1. Put all fixings into your bread machine, carefully following the instructions of the manufacturer
2. Set the program of your bread machine to Basic/White Bread and set crust type to Medium. Press starts.
3. Wait until the cycle completes. Once the loaf is ready, take the bucket out and let the loaf cool within 5 minutes. Shake the bucket to remove the loaf. Transfer, slice, and serve.

Nutrition:

Calories: 156 Fat: 8 g

Carbohydrates: 17 g Protein: 5 g

38. Zucchini Herbed Bread

Zucchini Herbed Bread is a sweet bread. The bread is tender with a nice crunchy crust and a soft middle.

Preparation Time: 2 hours 20 minutes

Cooking time: 50 minutes

Servings: 1 loaf

Ingredients:

- ½ cup of water
- 2 teaspoon honey
- 1 tablespoons oil

- ¾ cup zucchini, grated
- ¾ cup whole wheat flour
- 2 cups bread flour
- 1 tablespoon fresh basil, chopped
- 2 teaspoon sesame seeds
- 1 teaspoon salt
- 1½ teaspoon active dry yeast

Directions:

1. Put all of the fixings to your bread machine, carefully following the instructions of the manufacturer. Set the program of your bread machine to Basic/White Bread and set crust type to Medium.
2. Press starts. Wait until the cycle completes. Once the loaf is ready, take the bucket out and let the loaf cool within 5 minutes. Shake the bucket to remove the loaf. Transfer to a cooling rack, slice then serve.

Nutrition:

Calories: 153 Fat: 1 g

Carbohydrates: 28 g Protein: 5 g

39. Potato Bread

Potato Bread is one of the favorite recipes. As they said, potato bread is the most comfortable bread that you can eat.

Preparation Time: 3 hours

Cooking time: 45 minutes

Servings: 2 loaves

Ingredients:

- 1 3/4 teaspoon active dry yeast
- 2 tablespoon dry milk
- 1/4 cup instant potato flakes
- 2 tablespoon sugar
- 4 cups bread flour
- 1 1/4 teaspoon salt
- 2 tablespoon butter
- 1 3/8 cups water

Directions:

1. Put all the liquid ingredients in the pan. Add all the dry ingredients, except the yeast. Form a shallow hole in the middle of the dry ingredients and place the yeast.
2. Secure the pan in the machine and close the lid. Choose the basic setting and your desired color of the crust. Press starts. Allow the bread to cool before slicing.

Nutrition:

Calories: 35

Carbohydrate: 19 g

Fat: 0 g

Protein: 4 g

40. Golden Potato Bread

Golden Potato Bread is a yellow, soft, and moist flatbread made from tangy potatoes and slightly salty.

Preparation Time: 2 hours 50 minutes

Cooking time: 45 minutes

Servings: 2 loaves

Ingredients:

- 2 teaspoon bread machine yeast
- 3 cups bread flour
- 1 1/2 teaspoon salt
- 2 tablespoon potato starch
- 1 tablespoon dried chives
- 3 tablespoon dry skim milk powder
- 1 teaspoon sugar
- 2 tablespoon unsalted butter, cubed
- 3/4 cup mashed potatoes
- 1 large egg, at room temperature
- 3/4 cup potato cooking water, with a temperature of 80 to 90 degrees F (26 to 32 degrees C)

Directions:

1. Prepare the mashed potatoes. Put the peeled potatoes in a saucepan. Pour enough cold water to cover them. Adjust the heat to high and boil.
2. Adjust to low, then continue cooking the potatoes until tender. Move the cooked potatoes to a bowl and mash.
3. Cover the bowl until the potatoes are ready to use—Reserve cooking water and cook until it reaches the needed temperature.
4. Put the bread pan's fixings in this order: potato cooking water, egg, mashed potatoes, butter, sugar, milk, chives, potato starch, salt, flour, and yeast.
5. Put the pan in the machine, then close the lid. Turn it on, then choose the Sweet setting and your preferred crust color. Start the cooking process. Gently unmold the baked bread and leave it to cool on a wire rack. Slice and serve.

Nutrition:

Calories: 90

Carbohydrate: 15 g

Fat: 2 g

Protein: 4 g

41. Onion Potato Bread

This bread is perfect for breakfast. The onions and potatoes add a lot of flavor and depth to the bread.

Preparation Time: 1 hour 20 minutes

Cooking time: 45 minutes

Servings: 2 loaves

Ingredients:

- 2 tablespoon quick rise yeast
- 4 cups bread flour
- 1 1/2 teaspoon seasoned salt
- 3 tablespoon sugar
- 2/3 cup baked potatoes, mashed
- 1 1/2 cup onions, minced
- 2 large eggs
- 3 tablespoon oil
- 3/4 cup hot water, with a temperature of 115 to 125 degrees F (46 to 51 degrees C)

Directions:

1. Put the liquid ingredients in the pan. Add the dry ingredients, except the yeast. Form a shallow well in the middle using your hand and put the yeast.
2. Place the pan in the m the lid, and turn it o.. express bake 80 settings and sta.. machine. Once the bread is cooked, leave it on a wire rack for 20 minutes or until cooled.

Nutrition:

Calories: 160

Carbohydrate: 44 g

Fat: 2 g

Protein: 6 g

42. Spinach Bread

This bread is low in carbohydrates and is an excellent source of iron. It's a little high in natural sugar, so you may need to adjust your recipe's sweetness depending on how many slices you eat.

Preparation Time: 2 hours 20 minutes

Cooking time: 40 minutes

Servings: 1 loaf

- Ingredients:
- 1 cup of water
- 1 tablespoon vegetable oil

- 1/2 cup spinach, drained, chopped
- 3 cups all-purpose flour
- 1/2 cup shredded Cheddar cheese
- 1 teaspoon salt
- 1 tablespoon white sugar
- 1/2 teaspoon ground black pepper
- 2 1/2 teaspoons active dry yeast

Directions:

1. Put all fixings according to the suggested order of manufacture. Set the white bread cycle.

Nutrition:

Calories: 121

Carbohydrate: 20.5 g

Fat: 2.5 g Protein: 4 g

43. Curd Bread

This bread is slightly tart and very good with butter and jam.

Preparation Time: 4 hours

Cooking time: 15 minutes

Servings: 12

Ingredients:

- ¾ cup lukewarm water
- 3 2/3 cups of wheat bread machine flour
- ¾ cup cottage cheese
- 2 tablespoon softened butter
- 2 tablespoon white sugar
- 1½ teaspoon of sea salt
- 1½ tablespoon sesame seeds
- 2 tablespoon dried onions
- 1¼ teaspoon bread machine yeast

Directions:

1. Place all the dry and liquid ingredients in the pan and follow the instructions for your bread machine.
2. Pay particular attention to measuring the ingredients. Use a measuring cup, measuring spoon, and kitchen scales to do so. Set the baking program to BASIC and the crust type to MEDIUM.
3. When the program has ended, take the pan out of the bread machine and cool for 5 minutes. Shake the loaf out of the pan. If necessary, use a spatula.
4. Wrap the bread with a kitchen towel and set it aside for an hour. Otherwise, you can cool it on a wire rack.

Nutrition:

Calories: 277

Carbohydrate: 48.4 g

Fat: 4.7g

Protein: 9.4 g

44. Curvy Carrot Bread

Curvy Carrot Bread is a tropical bread that is soft but not powdery, and it has a subtle touch of sweetness and a mild taste of sun rays.

Preparation Time: 2 hours

Cooking time: 15 minutes

Servings: 12

Ingredients:

- ¾ cup milk, lukewarm
- 3 tablespoons butter, melted at room temperature
- 1 tablespoon honey
- ¾ teaspoon ground nutmeg
- ½ teaspoon salt
- 1 ½ cups shredded carrot
- 3 cups white bread flour
- 2 ¼ teaspoons bread machine or active dry yeast

Directions:

1. Take 1 ½ pound size loaf pan and add the liquid ingredients and then add the dry ingredients. Place the loaf pan in the machine and close its top lid.
2. Plug the bread machine into the power socket. For selecting a bread cycle, press Quick Bread/Rapid Bread, and choose a crust type, press Light or Medium.
3. Start the machine, and it will start preparing the bread. After the bread loaf is completed, open the lid and take out the loaf pan.
4. Allow the pan to cool down for 10-15 minutes on a wire rack. Gently shake the pan and remove the bread loaf. Make slices and serve.

Nutrition:

Calories: 142 Carbohydrate: 32.2 g

Fat: 0.8 g Protein: 2.33 g

45. Potato Rosemary Bread with Honey

This bread is easy to make and is perfect for sandwiches or soup.

Preparation Time: 3 hours

Cooking time: 30 minutes

Servings: 20

Ingredients:

- 4 cups bread flour, sifted

- 1 tablespoon white sugar
- 1 tablespoon sunflower oil
- 1½ teaspoons salt
- 1½ cups lukewarm water
- 1 teaspoon active dry yeast
- ½ tbsp honey
- 1 cup potatoes, mashed
- 2 teaspoons crushed rosemary

Directions:

1. Prepare all of the ingredients for your bread and measuring means (a cup, a spoon, kitchen scales). Carefully measure the ingredients into the pan, except the potato and rosemary.
2. Place all fixings into the bread bucket in the right order, following the manual for your bread machine. Close the cover.
3. Select the program of your bread machine to Bread with Fillings and choose the crust color to Medium. Press Start.
4. After the signal, put your mashed potato and rosemary into the dough. Wait until the program completes.
5. When done, take the bucket out and let it cool for 5-10 minutes. Shake the loaf from the pan and let cool for 30 minutes on a cooling rack. Slice, serve, and enjoy the taste of fragrant homemade bread.

Nutrition:

Calories: 106

Carbohydrate: 21 g

Fat: 1 g

Protein: 2.9 g

46. Beetroot Prune Bread

This bread is a slow rise bread enriched with prunes.

Preparation Time: 3 hours

Cooking time: 30 minutes

Servings: 20

Ingredients:

- 1½ cups lukewarm beet broth
- 5¼ cups all-purpose flour
- 1 cup beet puree
- 1 cup prunes, chopped
- 4 tablespoons extra virgin olive oil
- 2 tablespoons dry cream
- 1 tablespoon brown sugar
- 2 teaspoons active dry yeast
- 1 tablespoon whole milk
- 2 teaspoons sea salt

Directions:

1. Prepare all of the ingredients for your bread and measuring means (a cup, a spoon, kitchen scales). Carefully measure the ingredients into the pan, except the prunes.
2. Place all fixings into the bread bucket in the right order, following the manual for your bread machine. Close the cover.
3. Select the program of your bread machine to Basic and choose the crust color to Medium. Press Start.
4. After the signal, put the prunes in the dough. Wait until the program completes. When done, take the bucket out and let it cool for 5-10 minutes.

5. Shake the loaf from the pan and let cool for 30 minutes on a cooling rack. Slice, serve, and enjoy the taste of fragrant homemade bread.

Nutrition: Calories: 443 Carbohydrate: 81.1 g

Fat: 8.2 g Protein: 9.9 g

47. Sun Vegetable Bread

This unusual bread is prepared with spices and dried vegetables, and the beetroot gives it a fantastic reddish shade.

Preparation time: 15 minutes

Cooking time: 4 hours

Servings: 8

Ingredients

- 2 cups wheat flour
- 2 cups whole-wheat flour
- 2 teaspoons panifarin
- 2 teaspoons yeast
- 1½ teaspoons salt
- 1 tablespoon sugar
- 1 tablespoon paprika dried slices
- 2 tablespoons dried beets
- 1 tablespoon dried garlic
- 1½ cups water
- 1 tablespoon vegetable oil

Directions:

1. Set the baking program, which should be 4 hours; crust color is Medium. Be sure to look at the dough's kneading phase to get a smooth and soft bun.

Nutrition: Calories 253 Fat 2.6g

Carbohydrate 49.6g Protein 7.2g

48. Tomato Onion Bread

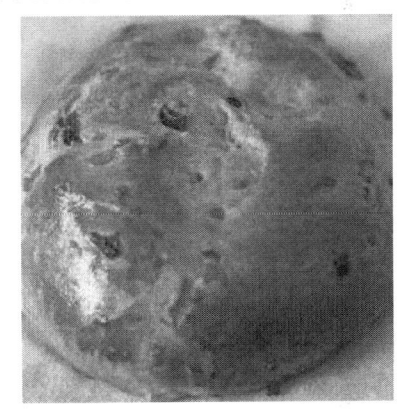

Enjoy this aromatic whole grain bread with vegetables.

Preparation time: 15 minutes

Cooking time: 4 hours

Servings: 12

Ingredients

- 2 cups all-purpose flour
- 1 cup whole meal flour
- ½ cup of warm water
- 4 ¾ ounces (140 ml) milk
- 3 tablespoons olive oil

- 2 tablespoons sugar
- 1 teaspoon salt
- 2 teaspoons dry yeast
- ½ teaspoon baking powder
- 5 sun-dried tomatoes
- 1 onion
- ¼ teaspoon black pepper

Directions:

1. Prepare all the necessary products. Finely chop the onion and sauté in a frying pan. Cut up the sun-dried tomatoes (10 halves).
2. Pour all liquid ingredients into the bowl; then cover with flour and put in the tomatoes and onions. Pour in the yeast and baking powder without touching the liquid.
3. Select the baking mode and start. You can choose the Bread with Additives program, and then the bread machine will knead the dough at low speeds. Enjoy!

Nutrition: Calories 241 Fat 6.4g

Carbohydrate 40g Protein 6.7g

49. Tomato Bread

This tomato bread has a magnificent orange color with a light note of tomato in taste. It is the best bread to serve with vegetables and fish.

Preparation time: 30 minutes

Cooking time: 3 hours

Servings: 8

Ingredients:

- 3 tablespoons tomato paste
- 1½ cups (340 ml) water
- 4 1/3 cups (560 g) flour
- 1½ tablespoon vegetable oil
- 2 teaspoons sugar
- 2 teaspoons salt
- 1 ½ teaspoons dry yeast
- ½ teaspoon oregano, dried
- ½ teaspoon ground sweet paprika

Directions:

1. Dilute the tomato paste in warm water. If you do not like the tomato flavor, reduce the amount of tomato paste, but putting less than 1 tablespoon does not make sense because the color will fade.
2. Prepare the spices. Sift the flour to enrich it with oxygen. Add the spices to the flour and mix well.
3. Pour the vegetable oil into the bread maker container. Add the tomato/water mixture, sugar, salt, the flour with spices, and then the yeast. Set to White Bread, then the crust is Medium.
4. When the baking cycle is finished, turn off the bread maker. Remove the bread container and take out the

hot bread. Place it on the grate for cooling for 1 hour. Enjoy!

Nutrition:

Calories 281

Fat 3.3g

Carbohydrate 54.3g

Protein 7.6g

50. Curd Onion Bread with Sesame Seeds

For lovers of onion bread, this is an airy, fragrant bread with plenty of onion notes.

Preparation time: 15 minutes

Cooking time: 4 hours

Servings: 8

Ingredients

- ¾ cup of water
- 3 2/3 cups wheat flour
- ¾ cup cottage cheese
- 2 tablespoons softened butter
- 2 tablespoon sugar
- 1 ½ teaspoons salt
- 1 ½ tablespoon sesame seeds
- 2 tablespoons dried onions
- 1 ¼ teaspoons dry yeast

Directions:

1. Put all the fixing in the bread machine according to its instructions. Bake on the Basic program.

Nutrition: Calories 277 Fat 4.7g

Carbohydrate 48.4g Protein 9.4g

51. Zucchini Carrot Bread

The basis for bread with young zucchini and carrots is prepared from three types of flour, which further enriches the taste. Its dough will be very wet and sticky; this will create a soft crumb.

Preparation time: 3 hours

Cooking time: 1 hour

Servings: 8

Ingredients:

- 1 small zucchini
- 1 baby carrot
- 1 cup whey
- 1 ½ cups white wheat flour

- ¾ cup whole wheat flour
- ¾ cup rye flour
- 2 tablespoons vegetable oil
- 1 teaspoon yeast, fresh
- 1 teaspoon salt
- ½ teaspoon sugar

Directions:

1. Dice carrots and zucchini to about 8-10 mm (1/2 inch) in size. In a frying pan, warm vegetable oil and fry the vegetables over medium heat until soft. If desired, season the vegetables with salt and pepper.
2. Transfer the vegetables to a flat plate so that they cool down more quickly. While still hot, they cannot be added to the dough.
3. Now dissolve the yeast in the serum. Put all kinds of flour, serum with yeast, and salt and sugar to the bakery.
4. Knead the dough in the dough for the Rolls program. At the very end of the batch, add the vegetables to the dough.
5. After adding vegetables, the dough will become moister. At the end of the fermentation process, which will last about an hour before doubling the dough's volume, shift it onto a thickly floured surface.
6. Form into a loaf and put it in an oiled form. Cover the form with a food film and leave for 1 to 1 1/3 hours.
7. Preheat oven to 450°F and put bread in it. Bake the bread for 15 minutes, and then gently remove it from the mold. Lay it on the grate and bake for 15-20 minutes more

Nutrition:

Calories 220 Fat 4.3g

Carbohydrate 39.1g Protein 6.6g

52. Olive Bread with Italian Herbs

Next time your craving for bread strikes, why not surprise your family with something different? This olive bread with Italian herbs is moist, tasty, and so pretty.

Preparation time: 15 minutes

Cooking time: 3 hours 50 minutes

Servings: 8

Ingredients:

- 1 cup (250 ml) water
- ½ cup brine from olives
- 4 tablespoons butter
- 3 tablespoons sugar
- 2 teaspoons salt
- 4 cups flour
- 2 teaspoons dry yeast
- ½ cup olives
- 1 teaspoon Italian herbs

Directions:

1. Add all liquid products. Then add the butter. Fill with brine and water. Add salt and sugar. Gently pour in the flour and pour the dry yeast in the corners on top of the flour.
2. Put the form in the bread maker and wait for the signal before the last dough kneading to add the olives and herbs.
3. In the meantime, cut olives into 2-3 parts. After the bread maker signals, add it and the Italian herbs into the dough.
4. Then wait again for the bread maker to signal that the bread is ready. Cooled bread has an exciting structure, not to mention the smell and taste. Bon Appetit!

Nutrition:

Calories 332 Fat 7.5g

Carbohydrate 55.5g Protein 7.9g

53. French Cheese Onion Bread

It is a very light, fragrant bread with a crispy crust and light, airy crumb.

Preparation time: 15 minutes

Cooking time: 6 hours

Servings: 8

Ingredients:

- 1 teaspoon dry yeast
- 3 ¼ cups bread flour
- 1 ¼ teaspoons salt
- 4/5 cup milk
- ½ cup Parmesan cheese
- 1 onion
- 1 tablespoon butter
- 1 tablespoon oil

Directions:

1. Grate the cheese on a fine grater. Minced the onion and fry in vegetable oil until it is transparent and soft.
2. In the bread maker's bucket, lay all the ingredients in the manner prescribed by the bread maker's instructions. Put the ready bread on a grate and cool it. Bon Appetit!

Nutrition:

Calories 260

Fat 6.5g

Carbohydrate 41.5g

Protein 8.2g

54. Italian Onion Bread

This bread is so wonderful, so absolutely loaded with onions, it just won't support a drizzle of olive oil. Instead, it's moist and mellow.

Preparation time: 15 minutes

Cooking time: 4 hours

Servings: 8

Ingredients:

- 2 ½ cups flour
- 1 ½ teaspoons salt
- 1 tablespoon sugar
- 1 teaspoon yeast
- 1 cup of water
- 2 big onions
- 3 tablespoons olive oil

Directions:

1. Cut onions (do not grind) and fry in olive oil until golden brown. At the end of frying, lightly powder with flour so that they become even more crispy.
2. Put in all products (except for onion and oil) following the bread maker's order and set the Basic program. Before the last batch, after the signal sounds, add the fried onions.

Nutrition:

Calories 209

Fat 5.7g

Carbohydrate 35g

Protein 4.6g

55. Carrot Oat Bread

This bread is a lovely and lighter variation to traditional carrot cake. Even those who have not enjoyed cooked carrots appreciate the addition of this refreshing sweet bread to their meal.

Preparation time: 15 minutes

Cooking time: 1 ½ hour

Servings: 8

Ingredients:

- ½ cup boiling water
- 2 carrots (1 1/3 cup carrot juice)
- 1/3 cup flour oatmeal

- 4 ½ cups wheat flour
- 1/3 cup sesame seeds
- 3 tablespoons sugar
- 3 tablespoons butter
- 3 tablespoons oat bran
- ½ teaspoon salt
- 2 teaspoons dry yeast

Directions:

1. Fry the bran in a dry frying pan and cool. Brew oatmeal with boiling water and leave to cool down too. Carrot juice is obtained by placing carrots in the juicer.
2. Add 2 tablespoons of carrot mill cake from the juicer to the dough. Pour all the ingredients, except for sesame, into the bread maker's bucket in the right order.
3. Now you can put the bucket into the bread maker. Select the Dough Mode. After the signal, add sesame seeds.
4. Bake on the Baking program for 1 hour. Serve the bread, Bon Appetit!

Nutrition:

Calories 403

Fat 8.5g

Carbohydrate 71.4g

Protein 10.2g

CHAPTER 9:

Cheese Bread

56. Cream Cheese Rolls

Cream Cheese Rolls is a cooked bread roll of the type often eaten for breakfast. They are slightly sweet and delicious. Everyone should know how to make them.

Preparation Time: 10 minutes

Cooking Time: 40 minutes

Servings: 6

Ingredients:

- 3 eggs
- 3 oz. Full-fat cream cheese, cubed and cold
- ¼ tsp. Cream of tartar
- ¼ tsp. salt

Directions:

1. Preheat the oven to 300F. Line a baking pan with parchment paper. Grease with cooking oil. Remove and separate the yolks from the eggs and place the whites in a container. Whisk with the tartar until stiff.
2. In another container, whisk the cream cheese, salt, and yolks until smooth.
3. Fold in the whites of the eggs, mixing well with a spatula. Mold a scoop of whites over the yolk mixture and fold together as you rotate the dish. Continue unit well combined.
4. Place six large spoons of the mixture onto the prepared pan. Mash the tops with the spatula to flatten slightly.
5. Bake until browned, about 30 to 40 minutes. Cool a few minutes in the pan. Then, carefully arrange them on a wire rack to cool.

Nutrition:

Calories: 91.3

Fat: 8g

Carb: 1g

Protein: 4.2g

57. Cheesy Garlic Bread

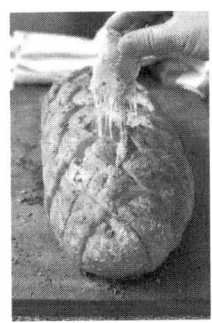

This bread is sure to score with the family! Make a quick homemade cheesy garlic bread that is easy to prepare in your bread machine and tastes great!

Preparation Time: 30 minutes

Cooking Time: 20 minutes

Servings: 10

Ingredients:

- 3/4 cup mozzarella, shredded
- 1/2 cup almond flour
- 2 tbsp cream cheese
- 1 tbsp garlic, crushed
- 1 tbsp parsley
- 1 tsp baking powder
- Salt, to taste
- 1 egg

For the toppings:

- 2 tbsp melted butter
- 1/2 tsp parsley
- 1 tsp garlic clove, minced

Directions:

1. Mix your topping fixings and set aside. Pour the remaining wet ingredients into the bread machine pan.
2. Add the dry ingredients—set the bread machine to the gluten-free setting. When the bread is done, remove the bread machine pan from the bread machine.
3. Let cool slightly before transferring to a cooling rack. Once on a cooling rack, drizzle with the topping mix. You can store your bread for up to 7 days.

Nutrition: Calories: 29 Carbohydrates: 1g

Protein: 2g Fat: 2g

58. Cheese Blend Bread

Cheese Blend Bread is an excellent way to use up pieces of cheeses leftover at the end of the week. It is a perfect bread, and there is nothing else quite like it. This recipe will make enough for a large family.

Preparation Time: 45 minutes

Cooking Time: 20 minutes

Servings: 12

Ingredients:

- 5 oz cream cheese
- 1/4 cup ghee

- 2/3 cup almond flour
- 1/4 cup coconut flour
- 3 tbsp whey protein, unflavored
- 2 tsp baking powder
- 1/2 tsp Himalayan salt
- 1/2 cup parmesan cheese, shredded
- 3 tbsp water
- 3 eggs
- 1/2 cup mozzarella cheese, shredded

Directions:

1. Place wet ingredients into bread machine pan. Add dry ingredients. Set the bread machine to the gluten-free setting.
2. When the bread is done, remove the bread machine pan from the bread machine. Let cool slightly before transferring to a cooling rack. You can store your bread for up to 5 days.

Nutrition:

Calories: 132 Carbohydrates: 4g

Protein: 6g Fat: 8 g

59. Parmesan Italian Bread

Parmesan Italian bread is very versatile and can be used for sandwiches or just as toast.

Preparation Time: 45 minutes

Cooking Time: 30 minutes

Servings: 10

Ingredients:

- 1 1/3 cup warm water
- 2 tbsp olive oil
- 2 cloves of garlic, crushed
- 1 tbsp basil
- 1 tbsp oregano
- 1 tbsp parsley
- 2 cups almond flour
- 1 tbsp inulin
- 1/2 cup parmesan cheese, grated
- 1 tsp active dry yeast

Directions:

1. Pour all wet ingredients into the bread machine pan. Add all dry ingredients to the pan. Set bread machine to French bread.
2. When the bread is done, remove the bread machine pan from the bread machine. Let cool slightly before transferring to a cooling rack. You can store your bread for up to 7 days.

Nutrition:

Calories: 150

Carbohydrates: 14g

Protein: 5g

Fat: 5g

60. Cheese Spinach Crackers

The plain taste gets into your head and stays there for a while. It can be served as a starter or as a snack. The cheese spinach crackers are very popular among children.

Preparation Time: 15 minutes

Cooking Time: 25 minutes

Servings: 16

Ingredients:

- 1 ½ cups almond flour
- 150g fresh spinach
- ½ cup flax meal
- ¼ cup coconut flour
- ½ tsp. ground cumin
- ¼ cup butter
- ½ cup parmesan cheese, grated
- ½ tsp. flaked chili peppers, dried
- ½ tsp. salt

Directions:

1. Bring water to boil in a saucepan. Add spinach and cook for 1 minute. Add cooked spinach leaves into a cold-water bowl to stop the cooking process.
2. Squeeze out the water from the spinach leaves and drain. Process the spinach in a food processor and process until a smooth consistency is reached.
3. In the meantime, add almond flour, coconut flour, flax meal, cumin, chili flakes, salt, and parmesan cheese into the bowl and mix well.
4. Add softened butter and spinach into the flour mixture and mix to combine well—transfer dough into a refrigerator. Wrap in foil and keep for 1 hour.
5. Preheat oven to 400F. Remove the foil wrapping and transfer the dough to a parchment paper-lined baking sheet.
6. Top dough with second parchment paper piece and roll dough with a rolling pin until the dough is ¼ inch thick.
7. Slice dough into 16 even pieces using a pizza cutter. Move baking sheet into the warm oven and bake dough for 18 to 20 minutes.
8. For a crunchier texture, adjust oven temperature to 260F and bake for 15 to 20 minutes more.

Nutrition:

Calories: 126

Fat: 10.9g

Carb: 1.4g

Protein: 4.5g

61. Cheesy Keto Sesame Bread

This bread is the ultimate keto bread recipe! It's crisp on the outside, soft and airy on the inside

Preparation Time: 5 minutes

Cooking Time: 30 minutes

Servings: 8

Ingredients:

- 1 tsp. sesame seeds
- 1 tsp. baking powder
- 1 tsp. salt
- 2 tbsp. ground psyllium husk powder
- 1 cup almond flour
- 4 tbsp. sesame or olive oil
- 7 ounces cream cheese
- 4 eggs
- Sea salt

Directions:

1. Preheat the oven to 400F. Beat the eggs until fluffy. Add cream cheese and oil until combined well. Set the sesame seeds aside and add the remaining ingredients.
2. Grease a baking tray. Spread the dough in the greased baking tray. Allow it to stand for 5 minutes. Baste dough with oil and top with a sprinkle of sesame seeds and a little sea salt.
3. Bake in the oven at 400F until the top is golden brown, about 30 minutes.

Nutrition:

Calories: 282

Fat: 26g

Carb: 2g

Protein: 7g

62. Ricotta Bread

This bread is healthier than the typical buttered bread because it's made from bread flour instead of wheat flour. It's delicious, easy to make, and goes great with any meal!

Preparation Time: 3 hours

Cooking Time: 30 minutes

Servings: 10

Ingredients:

- 1/3 cup milk
- 1 cup ricotta cheese
- 2 tablespoons butter
- 1 egg

- 2 ½ tablespoons sugar
- 1 teaspoon salt
- 2 ¼ cups bread flour
- 1 ½ teaspoons yeast

Directions:

1. Put all bread fixings in your bread machine, in the order listed above, starting with the milk, and finishing with the yeast.
2. Create or make a well in the center of your flour and place the yeast in the well. Make sure the well doesn't touch any liquid. Set the bread machine to the basic function with a light crust.
3. Check on the dough after about 5 minutes and make sure that it's a softball. Put water 1 tablespoon at a time if it's too dry, and add flour 1 tablespoon if it's too wet. When the bread is done, allow it cool on a wire rack.

Nutrition: Calories: 115 Fat: 6.5 g

Carbs: 3.3 g Protein: 8.5 g

63. American Cheese Beer Bread

American Cheese Beer Bread is a soft, moist bread that is perfect served with soup or your favorite sandwich filling. It does make a large loaf, so one slice is plenty.

Preparation time: 5 minutes

Cooking time: 60 minutes

Servings: 8

Ingredients:

- 1 ½ cups of fine almond flour
- 3 tsp unsalted melted butter
- salt, one teaspoon
- 1 egg
- 2 tsp sweetener
- 1 cup of keto low-carb beer
- ¾ tsp of baking powder
- ½ cup of cheddar cheese, shredded
- ½ tsp of active dry yeast

Directions

1. Prepare a mixing container, where you will combine the almond flour, swerve sweetener, salt, shredded cheddar cheese, and baking powder.
2. Prepare another mixing container, where you will combine the unsalted melted butter, egg, and low-carb keto beer.
3. As per the instructions on your machine's manual, pour the ingredients in the bread pan, taking care to follow how to mix in the yeast.
4. Place the bread pan in the machine, select the basic bread setting, together with the bread size and crust type, if available, then press start once you have closed the machine's lid.

5. When the bread is ready, using oven mitts, remove the bread pan from the machine. Use a stainless spatula to extract the pan's bread and turn the pan upside down on a metallic rack where the bread will cool off before slicing it.

Nutrition:

Calories: 80

Fat: 1.5g

Carb: 13g

Protein: 3g

64. Bacon Jalapeño Cheesy Bread

This bread is heaty! It's got an excellent salty heat from the bacon, the pepper's bite, and the savory of the cheese.

Preparation time: 5 minutes

Cooking time: 40 minutes

Servings: 12

Ingredients:

- 1 cup golden flaxseed, ground
- 3/4 cup coconut flour
- 2 tsp baking powder
- 1/4 tsp black pepper
- 1 tbsp erythritol
- 1/3 cup pickled jalapeno
- 8 oz cream cheese, full fat
- 4 eggs
- 3 cups shredded sharp cheddar cheese, + 1/4 cup extra for the topping
- 3 tbsp parmesan cheese, grated
- 1 1/4 cup almond milk
- 5 bacon slices (cooked and crumbled)
- 1/4 cup rendered bacon grease (from frying the bacon)

Directions:

1. Cook the bacon in a larger frying pan, set aside to cool on paper towels. Save 1/4 cup of bacon fat for the recipe; allow to cool slightly before using.
2. Add wet ingredients to the bread machine pan, including the cooled bacon grease. Add in the remaining ingredients.
3. When the bread is done, set to a quick bread setting, remove the bread machine pan from the bread machine.
4. Let cool slightly before transferring to a cooling rack. Once on a cooling rack, top with the remaining cheddar cheese. You can store your bread for up to 7 days.

Nutrition:

Calories: 235 Carbohydrates: 5g

Protein: 11g Fat: 17g

65. Cheese Jalapeno Bread

Cheese Jalapeno Bread is a sweet, somewhat spicy bread made with cheese. It is an easy loaf to make, and the results are well worth the effort.

Preparation Time: 5 Minutes

Cooking Time: 2 Hours

Servings: 10

Ingredients:

- ¼ cup shredded Monterey jack cheese
- 2 tsp active dry yeast
- 1 ½ tbsp butter
- 1 ½ tbsp sugar
- 3 tbsp milk
- 3 cups flour
- 1 cup water, or more
- 1 jalapeno pepper, minced
- 1 ½ tsp salt

Directions:

1. Begin by adding all fixings to the bread machine pan according to the bread machine manufacturer's instructions.
2. Select basic bread setting, then select light/medium crust and start. Once the loaf is done, remove the loaf pan from the machine. Allow it to cool for 10 minutes. Slice and serve.

Nutrition:

Calories 174

Carbs 31.1g

Fat 3.1g

Protein 5.1g

CHAPTER 10:

Savory Breads

66. Cream Cheese Bread

It is an excellent base for making fruit bread or chocolate chip bread.

Preparation time: 10 minutes

Cooking time: 4 hours

Servings: 12 slices

Ingredients:

- ¼ cup butter, unsalted
- 1 cup and 3 tbsp. cream cheese softened
- 4 egg yolks
- 1 tsp. vanilla extract
- 1 tsp baking powder
- ¼ tsp. sea salt
- 2 tbsp. monk fruit powder
- ½ cup peanut flour

Directions:

1. Add butter and cream cheese until combined. Then beat in egg yolks, vanilla, baking powder, salt, and monk fruit powder and mix well.
2. Add the egg mixture into the bread bucket, then top with flour, and shut the lid. Select the Basic/white cycle or low-carb setting and press Start. Remove the bread when done. Cool, slice, and serve.

Nutrition: Calories: 98 Fat: 7.9g

Carb: 2.2g Protein: 3.5g

67. Lemon Poppy Seed Bread

This bread is lemony-poppy-seed perfect! These delightful poppy seed gems can be enrobed in a glistening vanilla lemon topping; they are like little bread pearls.

Preparation time: 10 minutes

Cooking time: 4 hours

Servings: 6

Ingredients

- 3 eggs

- 1 ½ tbsp. butter, unsalted and melted
- 1 ½ tbsp. lemon juice
- 1 lemon, zested
- 1 ½ cups almond flour
- ¼ cup erythritol sweetener
- ¼ tsp. baking powder
- 1 tbsp. poppy seeds

Directions

1. Beat eggs, butter, lemon juice, and lemon zest until combined. In another bowl, add flour, sweetener, baking powder, and poppy seeds and mix well.
2. Add the egg mixture into the bread pan, top with flour mixture, and cover. Select the Basic/White cycle or low-car setting and press Start. Remove the bread when done. Cool, slice, and serve.

Nutrition: Calories: 201 Fat: 17.5g

Carb: 2.8g Protein: 8.2g

68. Cauliflower and Garlic Bread

It is perfect for the times that you have a lot of cauliflower and garlic to use up. This bread is golden brown with flecks of green in it. It is spongy but yet dense with a crisp crust.

Preparation time: 10 minutes

Cooking time: 4 hours

Servings: 9

Ingredients:

- 5 eggs, separated
- 2/3 cup coconut flour
- 1 ½ cup rice cauliflower
- 1 tsp minced garlic
- ½ tsp sea salt
- ½ tbsp chopped rosemary
- ½ tbsp chopped parsley
- ¾ tbsp baking powder
- 3 tbsp. butter, unsalted

Directions:

1. Put the cauliflower rice in your bowl and cover it. Microwave for 3 to 4 minutes or until steaming. Then drain. Wrap in cheesecloth and remove as much moisture as possible. Set aside.
2. Place egg whites in a bowl and whisk until stiff peaks form. Then transfer ¼ of the whipped egg whites into a food processor. Add remaining ingredients except for cauliflower and pulse for 2 minutes until blended.
3. Add cauliflower rice, and pulse for 2 minutes until combined. Then pulse in remaining egg whites until just mixed.
4. Add batter into the bread bucket and cover. Select the Basic/white cycle or low-carb. Press Start. Remove the bread when done. Cool, slice, and serve.

Nutrition: Calories: 108 Fat: 8g

Carb: 3g Protein: 6g

69. Almond Meal Bread

Almond Meal Bread is a type of bread that has been around in the market for some time. It has also been in the market at various bakeries.

Preparation time: 10 minutes

Cooking time: 4 hours

Servings: 10 slices

Ingredients:

- 4 eggs
- ¼ cup melted coconut oil
- 1 tbsp. apple cider vinegar
- 2 ¼ cups almond meal
- 1 tsp. baking soda
- ¼ cup ground flaxseed meal
- 1 tsp. onion powder
- 1 tbsp. minced garlic
- 1 tsp. sea salt
- 1 tsp. chopped sage leaves
- 1 tsp. fresh thyme
- 1 tsp. chopped rosemary leaves

Directions:

1. In a bowl, beat eggs, coconut oil, and vinegar until mixed. In another bowl, place an almond meal and add the remaining ingredients. Mix well.
2. Add the egg mixture into the bread bucket, and top with flour mixture. Cover the lid. Select the Basic/White cycle or low-carb. Press Start. Remove the bread when done. Cool, slice, and serve.

Nutrition:

Calories: 104

Fat: 8.8g

Carb: 2.1g

Protein: 4g

70. Macadamia Nut Bread

Macadamia Nut Bread is full of wonderful texture and flavor, and the macadamia nuts are the star of this show. Creamy and rich, this bread is a little more of a treat than sandwich bread.

Preparation time: 10 minutes

Cooking time: 4 hours

Servings: 8 slices

Ingredients:

- 1 cup natural macadamia nut butter
- 5 eggs

- ½ tsp. apple cider vinegar
- ¼ cup coconut flour
- ½ tsp. baking soda

Directions:

1. Mix macadamia nut butter, eggs, and vanilla and mix until smooth. Stir in flour and baking soda and mix well. Add the batter into the bread bucket and cover.
2. Select Basic/White cycle or low-carb. Press Start. Remove the bread when done. Cool, slice, and serve.

Nutrition:

Calories: 155

Fat: 14.3g

Carb: 3.9g

Protein: 5.6g

71. 3-Seed Bread

This bread is perfect for a dinner party appetizer or as an addition to any dinner spread. The crunchy crust will satisfy any appetite and conversation at the same time. That is, of course, if anybody feels like talking while they are eating this delicious bread.

Preparation time: 10 minutes

Cooking time: 4 hours

Servings: 18 slices

Ingredients:

2 eggs

- ¼ cup butter, melted
- 1 cup of warm water (100F)
- ¼ cup chia seeds
- ½ cup pumpkin seeds
- ½ cup psyllium husks
- ½ cup sunflower seeds
- ¼ cup coconut flour
- ¼ tsp. salt
- 1 tsp. baking powder

Directions:

1. Beat eggs and butter in a bowl until well blended. Add flour to another bowl. Then stir in the remaining ingredients except for water until mixed.
2. Pour water into the bread bucket, add egg mixture, and top with flour mixture, then cover.
3. Select the Basic/White cycle or low-carb. Press Start. Remove the bread when done. Cool, slice, and serve.

Nutrition:

Calories: 139

Fat: 10g

Carb: 5.6g

Protein: 5g

72. Cumin Bread

Cumin Bread is a slightly sweet bread with a prominent, but not overpowering, cumin flavor.

Preparation time: 10 minutes

Cooking time: 4 hours

Servings: 12 slices

Ingredients:

- 2 eggs
- 1 ½ tbsp. avocado oil
- 2/3 cup coconut milk, unsweetened
- 2 tbsp. Picante sauce
- 1 cup almond flour
- ½ cup coconut flour
- ¼ tsp salt
- 1 tbsp baking powder
- ¼ tsp. mustard powder
- 2 tsp. ground cumin

Directions:

1. Mix the eggs until frothy, then beat in oil, milk, and sauce until combined. In another bowl, place flours, then stir in remaining ingredients and mix.
2. Add egg mixture into the bread bucket, top with flour mixture, then cover. Select the Basic/White cycle or low-carb. Press Start. Remove the bread when done. Cool, slice, and serve.

NutritionCalories: 108 Fat: 8.3g

Carb: 4g Protein: 3.7g

73. Basic Rosemary Bread

Rosemary Bread is excellent to eat as a toast. You can also eat this bread as a snack with tea or coffee or even as a sandwich. You will feel your senses tingling with this aromatic bread.

Preparation time: 10 minutes

Cooking time: 4 hours

Servings: 10 slices

Ingredients:

- 6 eggs
- 8 tbsp. butter, unsalted and melted

- ½ cup coconut flour
- 1 tsp baking powder
- ¼ tsp salt
- ½ tsp onion powder
- 1 tsp garlic powder
- 2 tsp dried rosemary

Directions:

1. Gently mix eggs and butter until well combined. Place flour in another bowl. Stir in the remaining ingredients until mixed.
2. Add egg mixture into the bread bucket and top with flour mixture, then cover. Select the Basic/White cycle or low-carb. Press Start. Remove the bread when done. Cool, slice, and serve.

Nutrition:

Calories: 147

Fat: 12.5g

Carb: 3.5g

Protein: 4.6g

74. Sesame and Flax Seed Bread

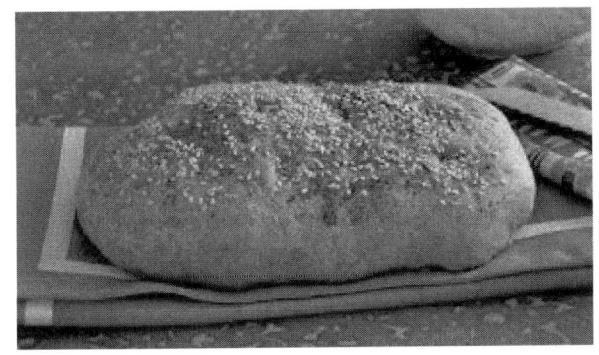

Sesame and Flax Seed Bread is a healthy and nutritious way to begin your day. This bread has a hearty texture, making the small amount of fat and fiber an excellent way to start your morning.

Preparation time: 10 minutes

Cooking time: 4 minutes

Servings: 10 slices

Ingredients:

- 3 eggs
- ½ cup cream cheese softened
- 6 ½ tbsp. heavy whipping cream
- ¼ cup melted coconut oil
- ½ cup almond flour
- ¼ cup flaxseed
- 6 ½ tbsp. coconut flour
- 2 2/3 tbsp sesame seeds
- ½ tsp salt
- 1 ½ tsp baking powder
- 2 tbsp ground psyllium husk powder
- ½ tsp ground caraway seeds

Directions:

1. Beat the eggs, cream cheese, whipping cream, and coconut oil until mixed. Add flours in another bowl. Then stir in the remaining ingredients and mix.
2. Add egg mixture into the bread bucket, then top with flour mixture, then cover. Select the Basic/White cycle or low-carb. Press Start. Remove the bread when done. Cool, slice, and serve.

Nutrition:

Calories: 230 Fat: 21g

Carb: 6.2g Protein: 6.3g

75. Dill and Cheddar Bread

This flavor combination is easily adaptable to suit your taste by increasing the number of cheddar cheeses or adding additional dill or other spices and herbs.

Preparation time: 10 minutes

Cooking time: 4 hours

Servings: 10 slices

Ingredients:

- 4 eggs
- ¼ tsp. cream of tarter
- 5 tbsp. butter, unsalted
- 2 cups grated cheddar cheese
- 1 ½ cups almond flour
- 1 scoop of egg white protein
- ¼ tsp salt
- 1 tsp garlic powder
- 4 tsp baking powder
- ¼ tbsp dried dill weed

Directions:

1. Beat eggs, cream of tartar, butter, and cheese until just mixed. Place flour in another bowl. Then stir in egg white protein, salt, garlic powder, baking powder, and dill and mix.
2. Add the egg mixture into the bread bucket, top with flour mixture, then cover. Select the Basic/White cycle or low-carb and press Start. Remove the bread when done. Cool, slice, and serve.

Nutrition:

Calories: 292

Fat: 25.2g

Carb: 6.1g

Protein: 14.3g

CHAPTER 11:

Meat Bread

76. French Ham Bread

French Ham Bread is a perfect, flaky pastry crust bread brimming with caramelized, salty ham and accentuated with parmesan cheese. The flavor and aroma are unique.

Preparation time: 15 minutes

Cooking time: 3 hours & 30 minutes

Servings: 10

Ingredients:

- 3 1/3 cups of wheat bread machine flour
- 1 cup ham, chopped
- ½ cup of milk powder
- 1½ tbsp. sugar
- 1 tsp. fresh yeast
- 1 tsp. kosher salt
- 2 tbsp. parmesan cheese, grated
- 1 1/3 cups lukewarm water
- 2 tbsp. extra-virgin olive oil

Directions:

1. Cut ham into cubes of ½ - 1 cm (approximately ¼ inch). Place all the dry and liquid ingredients in the pan and follow the instructions for your bread machine.
2. Set the baking program to French bread and, therefore, the crust type to Medium.
3. Add the additives after the beep or place them in the dispenser of the bread machine. If your dough is dense or too wet, adjust the recipe's quantity of flour and liquid.
4. When the program has ended, take the pan out of the bread machine and cool for five minutes.
5. Shake the loaf out of the pan. If necessary, use a spatula. Wrap the bread with a kitchen towel and set it aside for an hour. Otherwise, you'll calm on a wire rack.

Nutrition:

Calories 287

Fat 5.5g

Carbohydrate 47.2g

Protein 11.4g

77. Chicken Bread

Chicken bread is not only delicious, but it's a great source of protein and excellent for children's health. Why not give it a try for yourself?

Preparation time: 15 minutes

Cooking time: 3 hours & 30 minutes

Servings: 10

Ingredients:

- 2 cups boiled chicken, chopped
- 1 cup lukewarm whole milk
- 3 cups of wheat bread machine flour, sifted
- 1 tbsp. bread machine yeast
- 1 whole egg
- 1 tsp. sugar
- ½ tbsp. sea salt
- 2 tbsp. extra-virgin olive oil

Directions:

1. Pre-cook the chicken. You'll use a leg or fillet. Separate the chicken from the bone and cut it into small pieces.
2. Place all the dry and liquid ingredients, except the chicken, in the pan, and follow the bread machine's instructions.
3. Set the baking program to Basic and, therefore, the crust type to Medium. Add the chicken after the beep or place them in the dispenser of the bread machine. If your dough is too dense or too wet, adjust the recipe's flour and liquid quantity. When the program has ended, take the pan out of the bread machine and cool for 5 minutes. Shake the loaf out of the pan. If necessary, use a spatula. Wrap the bread with a kitchen towel and set it aside for an hour. Otherwise, you'll calm on a wire rack.

Nutrition: Calories 283 Fat 6.2g

Carbohydrate 38.4g Protein 17.2g

78. Onion Bacon Bread

Onion Bacon Bread is a way of taking everything you can make out of an onion, spreading it on bread, and adding bacon. It is a culinary delight that mustn't be missed - though those with weak stomachs are not recommended to eat it. Preparation time: 15 minutes

Cooking time: 3 hours

Servings: 12

Ingredients:

- 1½ cups lukewarm water

- 2 tbsp. sugar
- 3 tsp. bread machine yeast
- 4½ cups bread machine flour
- 1 whole egg
- 2 tsp. sea salt
- 1 tbsp. extra-virgin olive oil
- 3 small onions, chopped
- 1 cup fried bacon, chopped

Directions:

1. Place all the dry and liquid ingredients, except additives, in the pan, and follow the instructions for your bread machine.
2. Set the baking program to Basic and, therefore, the crust type to Medium. Add the additives after the beep or place them in the dispenser of the bread machine.
3. If your dough is too dense or too wet, adjust the recipe's flour and liquid quantity. When the program has ended, take the pan out of the bread machine and cool for five minutes.
4. Shake the loaf out of the pan. If necessary, use a spatula. Wrap the bread with a kitchen towel and set it aside for an hour. Otherwise, you'll calm on a wire rack.

Nutrition:

Calories 391

Fat 9.7g

Carbohydrate 59.9g

Protein 14.7g

79. Beef and Parmesan Bread

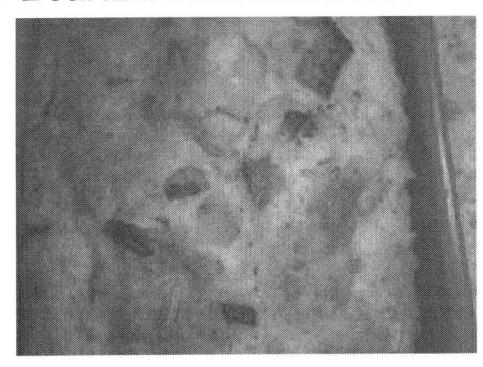

Bread with Beef and Parmesan is an innovation in bread making. It is an innovative way to have some great tasting bread whenever you please.

Preparation time: 1 hour

Cooking time: 1 hour

Servings: 6

Ingredients:

- 10 oz beef
- 1 cup of Parmesan cheese, grated
- 1 cup of wheat flour
- 1 cup of rye flour
- 2 onions
- 3 teaspoons dry yeast
- 5 tablespoons olive oil
- Sea salt to taste
- black pepper to taste
- red pepper to taste
- 1 teaspoon basilica

Directions:

1. Pour the warm water into the wheat flour and rye flour and leave overnight. Sprinkle the yeast with the sugar and set aside for 10 minutes.

Minced the onions, then cut the beef into small cubes.
2. In a skillet or wok, fry the beef chunks on low heat for around 20 minutes until soft and then mix in the onions and fry until transparent and caramelized.
3. Combine the yeast with the warm water, mixing until smooth consistency, and then combine the yeast with the flour, salt, and basilica, but don't forget to mix and knead well.
4. Add in the fried onions with the beef chunks, Parmesan cheese, black and red pepper, and mix well.
5. Pour some oil into a bread machine and place the dough into the bread maker. Cover the dough with the towel and leave for 1 hour.
6. Close the lid and turn the bread machine on the basic/white bread program.
7. Bake the meat bread until the medium crust, and after the bread is ready, take it out and leave for 1 hour covered with the towel, and slice the bread.

Nutrition:

Calories: 110

Carbs: 14g

Fat: 6g

Protein: 2g

80. Bacon and Walnuts Rye Bread

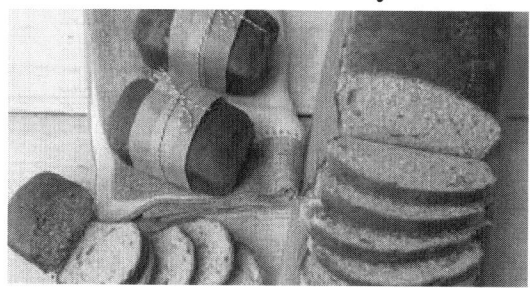

Bacon and Walnuts Rye Bread is a perfect recipe for the bread machine. This delicious combination of bacon and nuts. It is both a good dinner bread and an excellent bread for sandwiches.

Preparation time: overnight & 1 hour

Cooking time: 60 minutes

Servings: 4

Ingredients:

- 7 oz bacon
- 1 cup of walnuts
- 2 big onions
- 15 oz rye flour
- 5 oz wheat flour
- 3 tsp. dry yeast
- 3 tbsp. olive oil
- 1 tbsp. sugar
- Sea salt

Directions:

1. Preheat the oven to 250-270F and roast the walnuts in the oven for 10 minutes until lightly browned and crispy and then set aside to cool completely. Then grind the walnuts using a food processor or blender.
2. Combine the wheat flour and rye flour and pour the warm water to

leave overnight. Chop the onions and cut the bacon into cubes.

3. Fry the onions until transparent and caramelized, and then add in the bacon and fry on low heat for around 20 minutes until soft or on medium heat for 15 minutes.
4. Combine the yeast with the warm water, mixing until smooth consistency and then combine the yeast with the rye and wheat flour, walnuts, salt, and sugar, and then mix and knead well.
5. Add in the fried onions with the bacon and mix well. Pour some oil into a bread machine and place the dough into the bread maker. Wrap the dough with the towel and leave for 1 hour.
6. Set to basic/white bread program. Bake the bread until the medium crust, and after the bread is ready, take it out and leave for 1 hour covered with the towel, then slice the bread.

Nutrition: Calories: 140 Carbs: 28g

Fat: 3g Protein: 5g

81. Turkey Breast Bread

This bread is best when made with leftover turkey breast, but you can use chicken or beef in place of the turkey if your family has a family tradition that doesn't include turkey.

Preparation time: 60 minutes

Cooking time: 60 minutes

Servings: 6

Ingredients:

- 1 smoked turkey breast
- 1 cup of Pecorino cheese, grated
- 2 cups of wheat flour
- 1 cup of rye flour
- 1 cup of raisins
- 10 oz bran
- 4 chopped cloves of garlic
- 2 onions
- 3 teaspoons dry yeast
- 1 cup of warm water
- 2 tablespoons powdered milk
- 2 tablespoons sugar
- 3 tablespoons olive oil
- sea salt
- black pepper

Directions:

1. Chop the onions and fry until transparent and caramelized. Cut the turkey breast into small pieces and combine them with the raisins. Combine all the ingredients and mix until smooth consistency.
2. Pour some oil into a bread machine and place the dough into the bread maker. Wrap the dough using a towel and leave for 1 hour.
3. Set to basic/white bread program. Bake until the medium crust, and

after the turkey bread is ready, take it out and leave for few hours on a grate and only then slice.

Nutrition:

Calories: 250

Carbs: 0g

Fat: 12g

Protein: 5g

82. Bread with Chicken, Apricots, and Raisins

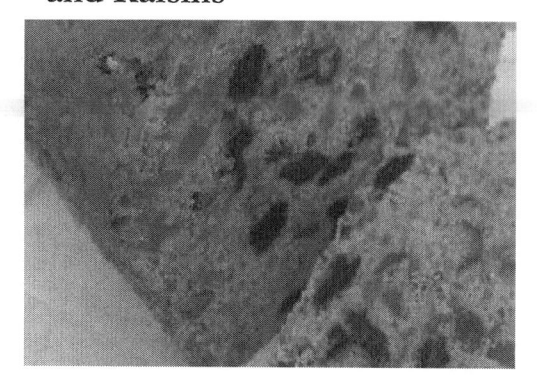

This bread is perfect for those who like eastern touches among their western recipes. Indeed a combination of tasty favorites!

Preparation time: 60 minutes

Cooking time: 1 hour & 10 minutes

Servings: 6

Ingredients:

- 10 oz chicken chunks
- 1 cup of apricots
- 1 cup of raisins
- 15 oz wheat flour
- 15 oz rye flour
- 4 chopped cloves of garlic
- 2 onions
- 3 teaspoons dry yeast
- 1 cup of warm milk
- 2 tablespoons sugar
- 3 tablespoons olive oil
- Sea salt
- ground black pepper

Directions:

1. Soak the apricots and raisins in the warm water for 10 minutes, and then cube the apricots. Chop the onions and fry until transparent and caramelized.
2. In a skillet or a wok, fry the chicken chunks for around 10 minutes. Combine all the ingredients and mix well.
3. Pour some oil into a bread machine and place the dough into the bread maker. Wrap the dough with the towel and leave for 1 hour. Set to basic/white bread program.
4. Bake until the medium crust, and after the bread is ready, take it out and leave for few hours on a grate and only then slice.

Nutrition:

Calories: 130

Carbs: 32g

Fat: 3g

Protein: 2g

83. Bread with Beef and Hazelnuts

This bread is so easy to make. You do not need to wait for raising, knead, or proofing. It is very healthy bread. This bread is very popular in the north of Italy in a region called Lombardia.

Preparation time: 60 minutes

Cooking time: 60 minutes

Servings: 6

Ingredients:

- 5 oz beef
- 1 cup of hazelnuts
- 15 oz wheat flour
- 5 oz rye flour
- 1 onion
- 3 teaspoons dry yeast
- 5 tablespoons olive oil
- 1 tablespoon sugar
- Sea salt
- ground black pepper

Directions:

1. Preheat the oven to 250-270 Fahrenheit and roast the hazelnuts in the oven for 10 minutes until lightly browned and crispy and then set aside to cool completely.
2. Then grind the hazelnuts using a food processor or blender.
3. Pour the warm water into the 15 oz of the wheat flour and rye flour and leave overnight.
4. Minced the onions and cut the beef into cubes.
5. Fry the onions until transparent and golden brown and then mix in the bacon and fry on low heat for 20 minutes until soft.
6. Combine the yeast with the warm water, mixing until smooth consistency, and then combine the yeast with the flour, salt and sugar, but don't forget to mix and knead well.
7. Add in the fried onions with the beef, hazelnuts, and black pepper and mix well.
8. Pour some oil into a bread machine, place the dough into the bread maker, wrap the dough with the towel, and leave for 1 hour.
9. Set to basic/white bread program. Bake the bread until the medium crust, and after the bread is ready, take it out and leave for 1 hour covered with the towel, then can slice the bread.

Nutrition:

Calories: 290

Carbs: 42g

Fat: 11g

Protein: 5g

84. Bread with Ham and Sausages

This bread is for all of you who like the taste of meat in your house. It comes out like a sticky bun or cake. It works well toasted. Guaranteed your family will love it.

Preparation time: 60 minutes

Cooking time: 60 minutes

Servings: 8

Ingredients:

- 8 oz ham
- 4 sausages, cubed
- 5 oz Herbes de Provence
- 10 oz wheat flour
- 10 oz rye flour
- 3 teaspoons dry yeast
- 5 oz warm water
- 1 cup of unsalted butter
- ½ half cup of olive oil
- Sea salt
- ground black pepper to taste

Directions:

1. Cut the ham into cubes. Fry the ham for 10-15 minutes on low heat until golden brown, and then mix in the cubed sausages.
2. Combine the unsalted butter with the Herbes de Provence, salt, pepper, and sifted flour, mixing until smooth consistency. Combine the flour mixture with the yeast and mix well.
3. Pour the warm water and the olive oil into the mixture and mix until the dough has a smooth consistency and homogenous mass. Stir in the fried ham and sausages and mix well.
4. Pour some oil into the bread machine and place the dough into the bread maker. Cover the dough with the towel and leave for 1 hour.
5. Set to basic/white bread program. Bake until the medium crust, and after the bread is ready, take it out and leave for few hours on a grate and only then slice.

Nutrition:

Calories: 124 Carbs: 18g

Fat: 1g Protein: 8g

85. Bread with Sausages and Celery

This bread is perfect for breakfast on a cold winter morning. It has just the right number of calories, and it's loaded with vital vitamins and minerals.

Preparation time: 60 minutes

Cooking time: 60 minutes

Servings: 8

Ingredients:

- 10 sausages
- 1 big celery, cubed
- 10 oz wheat flour

- 10 oz rye flour
- 3 teaspoon dry yeast
- 5 oz warm water
- 1 cup of unsalted butter
- 5 tablespoons olive oil
- Sea salt
- ground black pepper

Directions:

1. Cut the sausages into rings. Fry the sausages for 10-15 minutes on low heat until golden brown and mix in the celery cubes to stew for around 20 minutes on low heat.
2. Combine the unsalted butter with the salt, pepper, and sifted flour, mixing until smooth consistency and homogenous mass. Combine the flour mixture with the yeast and mix well.
3. Pour the warm water and the olive oil into the mixture and mix until the dough has a smooth consistency. Add the fried sausages with the celery and mix well.
4. Pour some oil into a bread machine and place the dough into the bread maker. Cover the dough with the towel and leave for 1 hour.
5. Set to basic/white bread program. Bake until the medium crust, and after the bread is ready, take it out and leave for few hours on a grate and only then slice.

Nutrition:

Calories: 254

Carbs: 25g

Fat: 16g

Protein: 4g

CHAPTER 12:

Grain, Seed and Nut Bread

86. Oat Bread

This bread is good any time of the day. It is like a heavy biscuit with a crusty outside. It is perfect when warm from the machine.

Preparation Time: 1 hour 30 minutes

Cooking Time: 40 minutes

Servings: 2-3 loaves

Ingredients:

- 1 cup oats
- 1 3/8 to 1½ cups water
- 2 tablespoons butter or margarine
- ¼ cup honey
- 2 teaspoons salt
- 3 cups bread flour red star brand
- 2 ½ tsp active dry yeast

Directions:

1. Put all fixings in the bread pan, then select medium crust setting and press start.
2. If it appears dry and stiff after 5 to 10 minutes, add more liquid 1 tablespoon at a time until dough forms a smooth, soft, pliable ball that is slightly tacky to the touch.
3. After the baking cycle ends, remove bread from pan, place on cake rack, and allow to cool 1 hour before slicing.

Nutrition:

Calories: 110

Carbohydrate: 19 g

Fat: 2 g

Protein: 4 g

87. Whole-Wheat Bread

This bread is healthier, and it keeps you pretty fit when you are eating it. It contains a lot of fiber and necessary vitamins.

Preparation Time: 1 hour 10 minutes

Cooking Time: 40 minutes

Servings: 1 loaf

Ingredients:

- 3/4 to 7/8 cup water
- 1 teaspoon salt
- 3 tablespoon butter or margarine
- 1 tablespoon Sugar
- 1 1/3 cups whole wheat flour
- 2/3 cups bread flour
- 3 tablespoon instant potato flakes
- 1 1/2 teaspoon Active dry yeast optional:
- 2 tablespoon vital wheat gluten

Directions:

1. Using the least amount of liquid indicated in the recipe, place all the ingredients in the bread pan. Select the medium crust, then the whole wheat cycle. Press starts.
2. After 5-10 minutes, observe the dough as it kneads; if you hear straining sounds in your machine or if the dough appears stiff and dry, add 1 tablespoon liquid at a time until the dough becomes smooth, pliable, soft, and slightly tacky to the touch.
3. Remove your bread from the pan after baking. Put on the rack and let it cool for 1 hour before slicing.

Nutrition:

Calories: 60 Carbohydrate: 11 g

Fat: 1 g Protein: 3 g

88. Golden Corn Bread

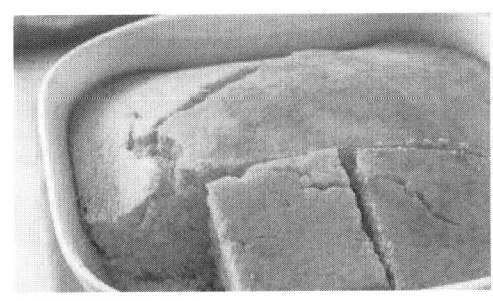

Golden Corn Bread is very delicious. You can put cooked bacon and cheese on top of it before you put it in the oven. This cornbread is delicious. It is also very good with french fries.

Preparation Time: 1 hour 10 minutes

Cooking Time: 50 minutes

Servings: 2 loaves

Ingredients:

- 1 cup buttermilk at 80 degrees F
- 2 whole eggs, at room temperature

- ¼ cup melted butter cooled
- 1 1/3 cups all-purpose flour
- 1 cup cornmeal
- ¼ cup of sugar
- 1 tablespoon baking powder
- 1 teaspoon salt

Directions:

1. Add buttermilk, butter, and eggs to your bread machine, carefully following the manufacturer's instructions. Program the device for quick/rapid bread mode and press start.
2. While the wet ingredients are being mixed in the machine, take a small bowl and combine it with flour, cornmeal, sugar, baking powder, and salt.
3. After the first fast mix is done and the machine gives the signal, add dry ingredients. Wait until the whole cycle completes.
4. Once the loaf is done, take the bucket out and let it cool for 5 minutes. Gently shake the basket to remove the loaf and transfer to a cooling rack. Slice and serve!

Nutrition:

Calories: 158

Fat: 5 g

Carbohydrates: 24 g

Protein: 4 g

89. Oatmeal Bread

This bread is exceptionally moist, even when toasted. It has a mild oatmeal flavor, with a slight sweetness, and can be great with any meal. It is very similar to a regular oatmeal cookie.

Preparation Time: 2 hours 10 minutes

Cooking Time: 50 minutes

Servings: 1 loaf

Ingredients:

- ¾ cup water at 80 degrees F
- 2 tablespoons melted butter, cooled
- 2 tablespoons sugar
- 1 teaspoon salt
- ¾ cup quick oats
- 1½ cups white bread flour
- 1 teaspoon instant yeast

Directions:

1. Put all fixings to your bread machine, carefully following the instructions of the manufacturer.
2. Set the program of your bread machine to Basic/White Bread and set crust type to Medium. Press starts. Wait until the cycle completes.
3. Once the loaf is ready, take the bucket out and let the loaf cool within 5 minutes. Shake the bucket

to remove the loaf. Move to a cooling rack, slice, and serve.

Nutrition:

Calories: 149

Fat: 4 g

Carbohydrates: 26 g

Protein: 4 g

90. Corn, Poppy Seeds, and Sour Cream Bread

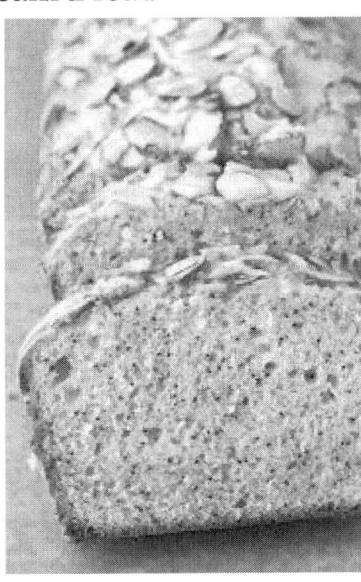

This bread is a simple recipe and a favorite for bread machines.

It is a combination of cornmeal, poppy seeds, and sour cream that gives it its texture and the zest of life it has.

Preparation Time: 2 hours 40 minutes

Cooking Time: 50 minutes

Servings: 2 loaves

Ingredients:

- 3½ cups wheat flour
- 1¾ cups of cornflour
- 5 ounces sour cream
- 2 tablespoons corn oil
- 2 teaspoons active dried yeast
- 2 teaspoons salt
- 16 ¼ ounces water
- Poppy seeds for sprinkling

Directions:

1. Add 16¼ ounces of water and corn oil to the bread maker bucket. Add flour, sour cream, sugar, and salt from different angles.
2. Make a groove in the flour and add yeast. Set the program of your bread machine to Basic/White Bread and set crust type to Medium. Press starts. Wait until the cycle completes.
3. Once the loaf is ready, take the bucket out and let the loaf cool within 5 minutes. Shake the bucket to remove the loaf.
4. Moisten the top using water and sprinkle with poppy seeds. Move to a cooling rack, slice, and serve.

Nutrition:

Calories: 374

Fat: 10 g

Carbohydrates: 64 g

Protein: 9 g

91. Grump's Special Bread

This bread is incredibly simple to make, and it never fails to delight.

Preparation Time: 2 hours 30 minutes

Cooking Time: 40 minutes

Servings: 1 loaf

Ingredients:

- 1 1/4 cups skim milk
- 1 cup crispy rice cereal
- 3 cups bread flour
- 2 tablespoons honey
- 1 1/4 teaspoons salt
- 1 1/2 packages active dry yeast
- 2 tablespoons margarine

Directions:

1. Into the bread machine pan, add the ingredients according to the order given by the manufacturer. Use the Basic/White Bread setting and then press the Start button. Serve.

Nutrition:

Calories: 46 Carbohydrate: 6.5 g

Fat: 1.9 g Protein: 1.4 g

92. Butter Honey Wheat Bread

Butter Honey Wheat Bread is easy to prepare in your bread maker and makes a yummy 1 loaf.

Preparation Time: 3 hours 5 minutes

Cooking Time: 15 minutes

Servings: 12

Ingredients:

- 1 cup of water
- 2 tablespoons margarine
- 2 tablespoons honey
- 2 cups bread flour
- 1/2 cup whole wheat flour
- 1/3 cup dry milk powder
- 1 teaspoon salt
- 1 (.25 oz.) package active dry yeast

Directions:

1. Follow the order of putting the ingredients into the bread machine recommended by the manufacturer. Run the bread machine for a large loaf (1-1/2 lb.) on a Wheat setting.

Nutrition:

Calories: 57 Carbohydrate: 8.5 g

Fat: 1.9 g Protein: 2.1 g

93. Buttermilk Wheat Bread

This bread is easy to make in your bread machine. It's great right out of the machine. If you use the light crust setting, you'll have a lovely, soft, golden-brown loaf of bread.

Preparation Time: 6 hours 8 minutes

Cooking Time: 15 minutes

Servings: 12

Ingredients:

- 1 1/2 cups buttermilk
- 1 1/2 tablespoons butter, melted
- 2 tablespoons white sugar
- 3/4 teaspoon salt
- 3 cups all-purpose flour
- 1/3 cup whole wheat flour
- 1 1/2 teaspoons active dry yeast

Directions:

1. In the bread machine pan, measure all ingredients in the order the manufacturer recommended. Set the machine to the Basic White Bread setting.
2. Start the machine. After a few minutes, add more buttermilk if the ingredients do not form a ball, or if it is too loose, put a handful of flour.

Nutrition:

Calories: 160

Carbohydrate: 30 g

Fat: 2.1 g

Protein: 4.9 g

94. Cracked Wheat Bread

Cracked Wheat Bread is a whole grain bread made with cracked wheat. This bread is simple to prepare in a bread machine.

Preparation Time: 3 hours 5 minutes

Cooking Time: 15 minutes

Servings: 12

Ingredients:

- 1 1/4 cups water
- 2 tablespoons margarine, softened
- 2 tablespoons dry milk powder
- 2 tablespoons brown sugar
- 1 1/4 teaspoons salt
- 3 cups bread flour
- 1/3 cup whole wheat flour

- 1/4 cup cracked wheat
- 1 1/4 teaspoons active dry yeast

Directions:

1. In the bread machine pan, measure all of the ingredients in the order the manufacturer suggested.
2. Choose regular/light cycle, then start. Serve.

Nutrition:

Calories: 50

Carbohydrate: 7.3 g

Fat: 1.9 g

Protein: 1.4 g

95. Flax and Sunflower Seed Bread

This bread is healthy and will provide you with good energy.

It is also tasty and convenient for people on the go (e.g., students).

Preparation Time: 3 hours

Cooking Time: 15 minutes

Servings: 15

Ingredients:

- 1 1/3 cups water
- 2 tablespoons butter, softened
- 3 tablespoons honey
- 1 1/2 cups bread flour
- 1 1/3 cups whole wheat bread flour
- 1 teaspoon salt
- 1 teaspoon active dry yeast
- 1/2 cup flax seeds
- 1/2 cup sunflower seeds

Directions:

1. With the manufacturer's suggested order, add all the ingredients (apart from sunflower seeds) to the bread machine's pan.
2. Select basic white cycle; press start. Just in the knead cycle that your machine signals alert sounds, add the sunflower seeds.

Nutrition:

Calories: 140

Carbohydrate: 22.7 g

Fat: 4.2 g

Protein: 4.2 g

96. High Flavor Bran Bread

High Flavor Bran Bread is a high fiber bread that contains 5 grams of fiber per slice. This high fiber bread is an excellent bread to use for shredding in recipes for bread stuffing.

Preparation Time: 3 hours

Cooking Time: 15 minutes

Servings: 15

Ingredients:

- 1 1/2 cups warm water at 110 F
- 2 tablespoons dry milk powder
- 2 tablespoons vegetable oil
- 2 tablespoons molasses
- 2 tablespoons honey
- 1 1/2 teaspoons salt
- 2 1/4 cups whole wheat flour
- 1 1/4 cups bread flour
- 1 cup whole bran cereal
- 2 teaspoons active dry yeast

Directions:

1. Put all fixings as directed by the machine's maker. Set the machine to either the whole grain or whole wheat setting.

Nutrition:

Calories: 146

Carbohydrate: 27.9 g

Fat: 2.4 g

Protein: 4.6 g

97. Honey and Flaxseed Bread

This bread is very tender because it's baked in a bread machine. Flaxseed is very high in Omega-3 and suitable for you.

Preparation Time: 3 hours

Cooking Time: 15 minutes

Servings: 12

Ingredients:

- 1 1/8 cups water
- 1 1/2 tablespoons flaxseed oil
- 3 tablespoons honey
- 1/2 tablespoon liquid lecithin
- 3 cups whole wheat flour
- 1/2 cup flax seed
- 2 tablespoons bread flour

- 3 tablespoons whey powder
- 1 1/2 teaspoons sea salt
- 2 teaspoons active dry yeast

Directions:

1. In the bread machine pan, put in all of the ingredients following the order recommended by the manufacturer. Choose the Wheat cycle on the machine and press the start.

Nutrition:

Calories: 174

Carbohydrate: 30.8 g

Fat: 4.9 g

Protein: 7.1 g

98. Honey Whole Wheat Bread

This bread is made from naturally sweet whole wheat flour; it does not get spoiled quickly and is great in sandwiches and even snacks.

Preparation Time: 3 hours 5 minutes

Cooking Time: 15 minutes

Servings: 10

Ingredients:

- 1 1/8 cups warm water (110 degrees F/45 degrees C)
- 3 tablespoons honey
- 1/3 teaspoon salt
- 1 1/2 cups whole wheat flour
- 1 1/2 cups bread flour
- 2 tablespoons vegetable oil
- 1 1/2 teaspoons active dry yeast

Directions:

1. Put the ingredients into the bread machine following the order recommended by the manufacturer. Choose the Wheat Bread cycle and the setting for Light Color on the machine.

Nutrition:

Calories: 180 calories;

Carbohydrate: 33.4 g

Fat: 3.5 g

Protein: 5.2 g

99. Maple Whole Wheat Bread

This bread is very hearty, and more importantly, it is full of vitamins, thanks to the whole wheat flour. The maple flavor makes for a sweet treat that can be enjoyed as a breakfast or a dessert.

Preparation Time: 3 hours 5 minutes

Cooking Time: 15 minutes

Servings: 10

Ingredients:

- 2 1/2 cups whole wheat flour
- 1/2 cup bread flour
- 1/3 teaspoon salt
- 1 1/4 cups water
- 4 tablespoons maple syrup
- 2 tablespoons olive oil
- 1 1/2 teaspoons active dry yeast

Directions:

1. Put the fixings into the bread machine pan following the order suggested by the manufacturer. Choose the Wheat Bread cycle on the machine and press the Start button.

Nutrition:

Calories: 144 Carbohydrate: 26.9 g

Fat: 2.8 g Protein: 4.3 g

100. Oat and Honey Bread

This bread is simply exquisite. It is soft and moist, it has a lovely flavor and just a touch of sweetness.

Preparation Time: 3 hours 5 minutes

Cooking Time: 15 minutes

Servings: 10

Ingredients:

- 1 cup buttermilk
- 1 egg
- 1/4 cup warm water (110 degrees F/45 degrees C)
- 2 tablespoons honey
- 1 1/2 cups whole wheat flour
- 1 1/2 cups all-purpose flour
- 1/2 cup quick-cooking oats
- 2 tablespoons vegetable oil
- 1 1/2 teaspoons salt
- 1 1/2 teaspoons active dry yeast

Directions:

1. Check all ingredients and place them into the bread machine according to the manufacturer's suggestion. Select Light Crust or Whole Wheat. Press Start.

Nutrition:

Calories: 200

Carbohydrate: 35 g

Fat: 4.3 g

Protein: 6.6 g

101. Nutty Bread

It is a delicious bread with an airy core and light crust.

Preparation time: 10 minutes

Cooking time: 3 hours

Servings: 12

Ingredients:

- 2 cups of bread flour
- 1¼ cups of water
- 1 cup of whole wheat flour
- ½ cup of regular or quick oatmeal
- ¼ cup of molasses
- ¾ cup of walnuts
- 1 tablespoon of oil
- 2¼ teaspoons of active dry yeast
- 1½ teaspoons of salt
- 1 teaspoon of lemon juice

Directions:

1. Put all fixings to your bread machine pan according to the order suggested by the manufacturer. Select quick or regular cycle and press start.

Nutrition: Calories: 181 Fat: 5.02 g

Carbohydrates: 30.44 g Protein: 4.75 g

102. Multi-Seed Bread

This loaf will leave you crunching happily.

Preparation time: 15 minutes

Cooking time: 3 hours

Servings: 16

Ingredients:

- 1½ cups of whole wheat flour
- 1¼ cups of bread flour
- 1¼ cups of water
- ¼ cup of sesame seed
- ¼ cup of shelled sunflower seeds
- ¼ cup of pumpkin seed
- 1/3 cup of rolled oats
- 2 tablespoons of poppy seed
- 2 tablespoons of honey
- 4 teaspoons of gluten flour
- 4 teaspoons of canola oil
- 2 teaspoons flax seed
- 1¼ teaspoons of active dry yeast
- ¾ teaspoon of anise seed
- ¾ teaspoon of salt

Directions:

1. Put all fixings to your bread machine pan according to the order suggested by the manufacturer. Select whole wheat or basic cycle and press start.

Nutrition:

Calories: 149

Fat: 5.87 g;

Carbohydrates: 21.35 g

Protein: 5.08 g

103. Barley Bread

It is hearty, moist, and filling.

Preparation time: 10 minutes

Cooking time: 3 hours

Servings: 15

Ingredients:

- 3 cups of bread flour
- 1½ cups of water
- 1 cup of barley flour
- ¼ cup of sunflower seeds
- 1 tablespoon of olive oil
- 2 teaspoons of brown sugar
- 1½ teaspoons of yeast
- 1 teaspoon of salt

Directions:

1. Put all fixings except the sunflower seeds into your bread machine pan according to the order suggested by the manufacturer.
2. Select dough or fruit and nut cycle and press start. Add the sunflower seeds when it beeps.

Nutrition:

Calories: 154

Fat: 2.55 g

Carbohydrates: 28.46 g

Protein: 4.32 g

104. Walnut Bread

Fluffy, and can be used as a sandwich or as a dip for soups.

Preparation time: 5 minutes

Cooking time: 4 hours

Servings: 16

Ingredients:

- 3 cups of bread flour

- 1 cup of water
- ¾ cup of walnuts, chopped and toasted
- 2 tablespoons of sugar
- 2 tablespoons of nonfat dry milk powder
- 1 egg
- 4½ teaspoons of soft butter
- 1½ teaspoons of active dry yeast
- 1 teaspoon of salt

Directions:

1. Put all fixings to your bread machine pan according to the order suggested by the manufacturer. Select basic bread setting and press start.

Nutrition:

Calories: 139 Fat: 4.39 g

Carbohydrates: 21.05 g Protein: 3.87 g

105. Peanut Butter Bread

Express your love for peanut butter with this protein-rich bread.

Preparation time: 5 minutes

Cooking time: 3 hours

Servings: 18

Ingredients:

- 1½ cups of bread flour
- 1½ cups of whole wheat flour
- 1¼ cups of water
- ½ cup of creamy or chunky peanut butter
- ¼ cup of brown sugar
- 3 tablespoons of gluten flour
- 2¼ teaspoons of active dry yeast
- ¼ teaspoon of salt

Directions:

1. Put all fixings to your bread machine pan according to the order suggested by the manufacturer. Select whole wheat setting and press start.

Nutrition:

Calories: 136

Fat: 4.34 g

Carbohydrates: 20.88 g

Protein: 4.77 g

CHAPTER 13:

Herbed and Spice Bread

106. Original Italian Herb Bread

This bread is excellent on its own or with various cheeses or as the basis for bruschetta. Or, when you just want some fresh bread, bake it in a small loaf pan.

Preparation Time: 15 minutes

Cooking Time: 3 hours

Servings: 20 slices

Ingredients:

- 1 cup water at 80 degrees F
- ½ cup olive brine
- 1½ tablespoons butter
- 3 tablespoons sugar
- 2 teaspoons salt
- 5 1/3 cups flour
- 2 teaspoons bread machine yeast
- 20 olives, black/green
- 1½ teaspoons Italian herbs

Directions:

1. Cut olives into slices. Put all ingredients into your bread machine (except olives), carefully following the manufacturer's instructions.
2. Set the program of your bread machine to French bread and set crust type to Medium. Once the maker beeps, add olives. Wait until the cycle completes.
3. Once the loaf is ready, take the bucket out and cool the loaf for 6 minutes. Wobble the bucket to take off the loaf.

Nutrition:

Calories: 386

Carbs: 71g

Protein: 10g

Fat: 7g

107. Aromatic Lavender Bread

This bread is adaptable. The lavender plays a significant role in the creation of the bread's signature aroma. Without the lavender, the bread will not smell or taste the same.

Preparation Time: 5 minutes

Cooking Time: 2 hours and 45 minutes

Servings: 8 slices

Ingredients:

- ¾ cup milk at 80 degrees F
- 1 tablespoon melted butter, cooled
- 1 tablespoon sugar
- ¾ teaspoon salt
- 1 teaspoon fresh lavender flower, chopped
- ¼ teaspoon lemon zest
- ¼ teaspoon fresh thyme, chopped
- 2 cups white bread flour
- ¾ teaspoon instant yeast

Directions:

1. Put all fixings to your bread machine, carefully following the instructions of the manufacturer. Set the program of your bread machine to Basic/White Bread and set crust type to Medium.
2. Wait until the cycle completes. Once the loaf is ready, take the bucket out and let the loaf cool within 5 minutes. Shake the bucket to remove the loaf.

Nutrition:

Calories: 144

Carbs: 27g

Protein: 4g

Fat: 2g

108. Cinnamon & Dried Fruits Bread

It is an excellent addition to any breakfast table. Warm out of the bread machine & spread with butter & you will be eating high on the food chain.

Preparation Time: 5 minutes

Cooking Time: 3 hours

Servings: 16 slices

Ingredients:

- 2 ¾ cups flour
- 1 ½ cups dried fruits
- 4 tablespoons sugar

- 2 ½ tablespoons butter
- 1 tablespoon milk powder
- 1 teaspoon cinnamon
- ½ teaspoon ground nutmeg
- ¼ teaspoon vanillin
- ½ cup peanuts
- powdered sugar, for sprinkling
- 1 teaspoon salt
- 1½ bread machine yeast

Directions:

1. Put all fixings into your bread machine (except peanuts and powdered sugar), carefully following the manufacturer's instructions.
2. Set the program of your bread machine to Basic/White Bread and set crust type to Medium. Once the bread maker beeps, moisten dough with a bit of water and add peanuts.
3. Wait until the cycle completes. Once the loaf is ready, take the bucket out and let the loaf cool within 5 minutes.
4. Shake the bucket to remove the loaf. Sprinkle with powdered sugar.

Nutrition:

Calories: 315

Carbs: 65g

Protein: 5g

Fat: 4g

109. Herbal Garlic Cream Cheese Delight

Herbal Garlic Cream Cheese Delight is a delightful treat for breakfast. It is simply addictive!

Preparation Time: 5 minutes

Cooking Time: 2 hours and 45 minutes

Servings: 8 slices

Ingredients:

- 1/3 cup water at 80 degrees F
- 1/3 cup herb & garlic cream cheese mix, at room temp
- 1 whole egg, beaten, at room temp
- 4 teaspoons melted butter, cooled
- 1 tablespoon sugar
- 2/3 teaspoon salt
- 2 cups white bread flour
- 1 teaspoon instant yeast

Directions:

1. Put all fixings into your bread machine, carefully following the instructions of the manufacturer.
2. Set the program of your bread machine to Basic/White Bread and set crust type to Medium. Wait until the cycle completes.

3. Once the loaf is ready, take the bucket out and let the loaf cool within 5 minutes. Shake the bucket to remove the loaf.

Nutrition: Calories: 182 Carbs: 27g

Protein: 5g Fat: 6g

110. Oregano Mozza-Cheese Bread

This bread is so moist and cheesy that you may have to use two spatulas to pull it out of the pan. The oregano and mozzarella add a sophisticated Italian flair to this comfort bread classic.

Preparation Time: 15 minutes

Cooking Time: 3 hours and 15 minutes

Servings: 16 slices

Ingredients:

- 1 cup (milk + egg) mixture
- ½ cup mozzarella cheese
- 2¼ cups flour
- ¾ cup whole grain flour
- 2 tablespoons sugar
- 1 teaspoon salt
- 2 teaspoons oregano
- 1½ teaspoons dry yeast

Directions:

1. Put all fixings to your bread machine, carefully following the instructions of the manufacturer.
2. Set the program of your bread machine to Basic/White Bread and set crust type to Dark. Wait until the cycle completes.
3. Once the loaf is ready, take the bucket out and let the loaf cool within 5 minutes. Shake the bucket to remove the loaf.

Nutrition: Calories: 209 Carbs: 40g

Protein: 7.7g Fat: 2.1g

111. Cumin Tossed Fancy Bread

Cumin Tossed Fancy Bread is a savory bread recipe for the Bread Machine that produces a delicious, crusty crust and soft interior.

Preparation Time: 5 minutes

Cooking Time: 3 hours and 15 minutes

Servings: 16 slices

Ingredients:

- 5 1/3 cups wheat flour

- 1½ teaspoons salt
- 1½ tablespoons sugar
- 1 tablespoon dry yeast
- 1¾ cups water
- 2 tablespoons cumin
- 3 tablespoons sunflower oil

Directions:

1. Add warm water to the bread machine bucket. Add salt, sugar, and sunflower oil. Sift in wheat flour and add yeast.
2. Set the program of your bread machine to French bread and set crust type to Medium. Once the maker beeps, add cumin. Wait until the cycle completes.
3. Once the loaf is ready, take the bucket out and let the loaf cool within 5 minutes. Shake the bucket to remove the loaf.

Nutrition: Calories: 368 Carbs: 67g

Protein: 9.5g Fat: 7g

112. Potato Rosemary Loaf

This bread is very flavorful and is an excellent complement to many soups and salads.

Preparation Time: 5 minutes

Cooking Time: 3 hours and 25 minutes

Servings: 20 slices

Ingredients:

- 4 cups wheat flour
- 1 tablespoon sugar
- 1 tablespoon olive oil
- 1½ teaspoons salt
- 1½ cups water
- 1 teaspoon dry yeast
- 1 cup mashed potatoes, ground through a sieve
- crushed rosemary to taste

Directions:

1. Add flour, salt, and sugar to the bread maker bucket and attach mixing paddle. Add olive oil and water. Put in yeast as directed.
2. Set the program of your bread machine to Bread with Filling mode and set crust type to Medium.
3. Once the bread maker beeps and signals to add more ingredients, open the lid, add mashed potatoes and chopped rosemary.
4. Wait until the cycle completes. Once the loaf is ready, take the bucket out and let the loaf cool within 5 minutes. Shake the bucket to remove the loaf.

Nutrition:

Calories: 276

Carbs: 54g

Protein: 8g

Fat: 3g

113. Honey Lavender Bread

This bread is scented with a light touch of the finest of lavender to make the most enchanting of scents while baking.

Preparation Time: 10 minutes

Cooking Time: 3 hours and 25 minutes

Servings: 16 slices

Ingredients:

- 1½ cups wheat flour
- 2 1/3 cups wholemeal flour
- 1 teaspoon fresh yeast
- 1½ cups water
- 1 teaspoon lavender
- 1½ tablespoons honey
- 1 teaspoon salt

Directions:

1. Sift both types of flour in a bowl and mix. Put all fixings to your bread machine, carefully following the instructions of the manufacturer.
2. Set the program of your bread machine to Basic/White Bread and set crust type to Medium. Wait until the cycle completes.
3. Once the loaf is ready, take the bucket out and let the loaf cool within 5 minutes. Shake the bucket to remove the loaf.

Nutrition:

Calories: 226

Carbs: 46g

Protein: 7.5g

Fat: 1.5g

114. Cinnamon Bread

This bread is fluffy, crusty, filling, flavorful, and can be frozen. It is so easy to make that all but the most hopeless of cooks can do it.

Preparation Time: 15 minutes

Cooking Time: 2 hours and 15 minutes

Servings: 8 slices

Ingredients:

- 2/3 cup milk at 80 degrees F
- 1 whole egg, beaten

- 3 tablespoons melted butter, cooled
- 1/3 cup sugar
- 1/3 teaspoon salt
- 1 teaspoon ground cinnamon
- 2 cups white bread flour
- 1 1/3 teaspoons active dry yeast

Directions:

1. Put all fixings to your bread machine, carefully following the instructions of the manufacturer.
2. Set the program of your bread machine to Basic/White Bread and set crust type to Medium. Wait until the cycle completes.
3. Once the loaf is ready, take the bucket out and let the loaf cool for 5 minutes. Remove the loaf.

Nutrition:

Calories: 198

Carbs: 34g

Protein: 5g

Fat: 5g

115. Lavender Buttermilk Bread

This bread is a breeze to make. The beautiful thing about this bread is the soft yet buttery crust and the rich dark color. You can slice this on your dinner plates just like good Italian bread.

Preparation time: 10 minutes

Cooking time: 3 hours

Servings: 14

Ingredients:

- ½ cup of water
- 7/8 cup buttermilk
- 1/4 cup olive oil
- 3 tablespoons finely chopped fresh lavender leaves
- 1 ¼ teaspoon finely chopped fresh lavender flowers
- Grated zest of 1 lemon
- 4 cups bread flour
- 2 teaspoon salt
- 2 3/4 teaspoon bread machine yeast

Directions:

1. Add each ingredient to the bread machine in the order and at the temperature recommended by your bread machine manufacturer.
2. Close the lid, select the basic bread, medium crust setting on your bread machine, and press start. When the bread machine has finished baking, remove the bread and put it on a cooling rack.

Nutrition:

Calories: 170 Carbs: 27 g

Fat: 5 g

Protein: 2 g

116. Cajun Bread

This bread is a lot like its creator, Cajun; it's so good. It's so easy. You won't believe it the first time you try it.

Preparation time: 10 minutes

Cooking time: 2 hours 10 minutes

Servings: 14

Ingredients:

- ½ cup of water
- ¼ cup chopped onion
- ¼ cup chopped green bell pepper
- 2 teaspoon finely chopped garlic
- 2 teaspoon soft butter
- 2 cups bread flour
- 1 tablespoon sugar
- 1 teaspoon Cajun
- ½ teaspoon salt
- 1 teaspoon active dry yeast

Directions:

1. Add each ingredient to the bread machine in the order and at the temperature recommended by your bread machine manufacturer.
2. Close the lid, select the basic bread, medium crust setting on your bread machine, and press start. When the bread machine has finished baking, remove the bread and put it on a cooling rack.

Nutrition:

Calories: 150

Carbs: 23 g

Fat: 4 g

Protein: 5 g

117. Turmeric Bread

Turmeric Bread is an excellent meal to be served at lunchtime. The bread is famous as it makes the stomach full and peaceful. Turmeric is also renowned as an antibacterial agent.

Preparation time: 5 minutes

Cooking time: 3 hours

Servings: 14

Ingredients:

- 1 teaspoon dried yeast
- 4 cups strong white flour
- 1 teaspoon turmeric powder

- 2 teaspoon beetroot powder
- 2 tablespoon olive oil
- 1 1/2 teaspoon salt
- 1 teaspoon chili flakes
- 1 3/8 water

Directions:

1. Add each ingredient to the bread machine in the order and at the temperature recommended by your bread machine manufacturer.
2. Close the lid, select the basic bread, medium crust setting on your bread machine, and press start. When the bread machine has finished baking, remove the bread and put it on a cooling rack.

Nutrition:

Calories: 129 Carbs: 24 g

Fat: 3 g

Protein: 2 g

118. Rosemary Cranberry Pecan Bread

This bread is delightful for breakfast, and it is a delicious treat when served with the main course as a bread accompaniment.

Preparation time: 30 minutes

Cooking time: 3 hours

Servings: 14

Ingredients:

- 1 1/3 cups water, plus
- 2 tbsp water
- 2 tbsp butter
- 2 tsp salt
- 4 cups bread flour
- 3/4 cup dried sweetened cranberries
- 3/4 cup toasted chopped pecans
- 2 tbsp non-fat powdered milk
- ¼ cup of sugar
- 2 tsp yeast

Directions:

1. Add each ingredient to the bread machine in the order and at the temperature recommended by your bread machine manufacturer.
2. Close the lid, select the basic bread, medium crust setting on your bread machine, and press start. When the bread machine has finished baking, remove the bread and put it on a cooling rack.

Nutrition:

Calories: 120

Carbs: 18 g

Fat: 5 g

Protein: 9 g

119. Sesame French Bread

This bread is light, buttery, and has a delicate sesame flavor. Use a bread machine to make it, and you will experience the pleasure of fresh-baked bread without kneading, fussing, or fumbling with a bread machine. Serve this bread with dinner or for brunch.

Preparation time: 20 minutes

Cooking time: 3 hours 15 minutes

Servings: 14

Ingredients:

- 7/8 cup water
- 1 tablespoon butter, softened
- 3 cups bread flour
- 2 teaspoon sugar
- 1 teaspoon salt
- 2 teaspoon yeast
- 2 tablespoon sesame seeds toasted

Directions:

1. Add each ingredient to the bread machine in the order and at the temperature recommended by your bread machine manufacturer.
2. Close the lid, select the French bread, medium crust setting on your bread machine, and press start. When the bread machine has finished baking, remove the bread and put it on a cooling rack.

Nutrition:

Calories: 180

Carbs: 28 g

Fat: 3 g

Protein: 6 g

120. Saffron Tomato Bread

This bread is eaten in the winter with soups and stews or hot toasted bread with butter and jam. Saffron has a subtle but expensive taste. On the other hand, it is considered as the well-being spice.

Preparation Time: 3 hours 30 minutes

Cooking Time: 15 minutes

Servings: 10

Ingredients:

- 1 teaspoon bread machine yeast
- 2½ cups wheat bread flour
- 1 tablespoon panifarin
- 1½ teaspoon kosher salt
- 1½ tablespoon white sugar
- 1 tablespoon extra-virgin olive oil
- 1 tablespoon tomatoes, dried and chopped
- 1 tablespoon tomato paste
- ½ cup firm cheese (cubes)
- ½ cup feta cheese
- 1 pinch saffron
- 1½ cups serum

Directions:

1. Five minutes before cooking, pour in dried tomatoes and 1 tablespoon of olive oil. Add the tomato paste and mix.
2. Place all the dry and liquid ingredients, except additives, in the pan and follow the instructions for your bread machine.
3. Pay particular attention to measuring the ingredients. Use a measuring cup, measuring spoon, and kitchen scales to do so.
4. Set the baking program to Basic and the crust type to Medium. Add the additives after the beep or place them in the dispenser of the bread machine.
5. Shake the loaf out of the pan. If necessary, use a spatula. Wrap the bread with a kitchen towel and set it aside for an hour. Otherwise, you can cool it on a wire rack.

Nutrition: Calories: 260 Carbohydrate: 35.5 g

Fat: 9.2g Protein: 8.9 g

121. Cracked Black Pepper Bread

This bread is rich in flavor and makes a good sandwich bread or a fine accompaniment for soup or a salad.

Preparation Time: 3 hours 30 minutes

Cooking Time: 15 minutes

Servings: 8

Ingredients:

- ¾ cup water, at 80 F-90 F
- 1 tablespoon melted butter, cooled
- 1 tablespoon sugar
- ¾ teaspoon salt
- 2 tablespoons skim milk powder
- 1 tablespoon minced chives
- ½ teaspoon garlic powder
- ½ teaspoon cracked black pepper
- 2 cups white bread flour
- ¾ teaspoon bread machine or instant yeast

Directions:

1. Put all fixings in your bread machine, as stated by the manufacturer. Set to Basic/White bread, select light or medium crust, and press Start.
2. When the loaf is done, remove the bucket from the machine. Let the loaf cool for 5 minutes. Gently shake the bucket to remove the loaf and turn it out onto a rack to cool.

Nutrition:

Calories: 141

Carbohydrate: 27 g

Fat: 2g

Protein: 4 g

122. Garlic, Herb, and Cheese Bread

This bread is delicious and makes for a beautiful snack and an excellent bread for sandwiches. The crisp texture of the bread and flavorful cheese, herbs, and garlic make for a mouthwatering combination.

Preparation Time: 5 minutes

Cooking Time: 45 minutes

Servings: 12

Ingredients:

- ½ cup ghee
- 6 eggs
- 2 cups almond flour
- 1 tsp baking powder
- ½ tsp xanthan gum
- 1 cup cheddar cheese, shredded
- 1 tbsp garlic powder
- 1 tbsp parsley
- ½ tbsp. oregano
- ½ tsp salt

Directions:

1. Lightly beat eggs and ghee before pouring into the bread machine pan. Add the remaining ingredients to the pan.
2. Set bread machine to gluten-free. When the bread is done, remove then cool slightly before transferring to a cooling rack.

Nutrition:

Calories 156

Carbohydrates 4 g

Fats 13 g

Protein 5 g

123. Onion Bread

This bread is suitable for a snack. It's easy to make, and the aroma of it baking is enjoyable.

Preparation time: 2 hours

Cooking Time: 15 minutes

Servings: 6

Ingredients:

- 5 oz beef
- 15 oz almond flour
- 5 oz rye flour

- 1 onion
- 3 teaspoons dry yeast
- 5 tablespoons olive oil
- 1 tablespoon sugar
- Sea salt
- Ground black pepper

Directions:

1. Pour the warm water into the 15 oz of the wheat flour and rye flour and leave overnight. Chop the onions and cut the beef into cubes.
2. Fry the onions until transparent and golden brown and then mix in the bacon and fry on low heat for 20 minutes until soft.
3. Combine the yeast with the warm water, mixing until smooth consistency, and then combine the yeast with the flour, salt and sugar, but don't forget to mix and knead well.
4. Add in the fried onions with the beef and black pepper and mix well. Pour some oil into a bread machine and place the dough into the bread maker. Wrap the dough using a towel and leave for 1 hour.
5. Close the lid and turn the bread machine on the basic/white bread program. Bake the bread until the medium crust, and after the bread is ready, take it out and leave for 1 hour covered with the towel, and only then can you slice the bread.

Nutrition: Calories 299 Carbohydrates 6 g

Fats 21 g

Protein 13 g

124. Spiced Cauliflower Buns

This bread is very light and fragrant; the cauliflower flavor doesn't overpowers the bread. The spices are very subtle. The bread is so good with spicy curries.

Preparation time: 10 minutes

Cooking time: 30 minutes

Servings: 8

Ingredients:

- 2 tablespoons coconut flour
- 1 tablespoon olive oil
- 1/4 teaspoon ground turmeric
- 2 cups chopped cauliflower
- 2 eggs
- A pinch each of salt & pepper

Directions:

1. Preheat your oven to 400 degrees. Set your loaf pan to prepare by lining it with parchment paper and greasing with cooking spray.
2. Process cauliflower in a food processor into 'rice'; steam the cauliflower rice until tender.
3. Transfer the steamed cauliflower to a bowl and mix in turmeric, eggs, olive oil, salt, and pepper until well blended; form buns from the mixture and arrange them onto a baking sheet. Bake for about 30 minutes or until light brown; serve hot.

Nutrition:

Calories: 187 Fat: 9.1 g

Carbs: 6.6 g

Protein: 4.5 g

125. Rosemary & Garlic Coconut Flour Bread

Rosemary & Garlic Coconut Flour Bread is a hearty bread that has a lot of health benefits. The bread is excellent for those who follow a low carb diet since it has low carbs and is also quite filling.

Preparation Time: 20 minutes

Cooking Time: 45 min

Servings: 4

Ingredients:

- 1/2 cup coconut flour
- 1 stick margarine
- 6 enormous eggs
- 1 tsp heating powder
- 2 tsp dried rosemary
- 1/2-1 tsp garlic powder
- 1/2 tsp onion powder
- 1/4 tsp pink Himalayan salt

Directions:

1. Mix dry fixings (coconut flour, heating powder, onion, garlic, rosemary, and salt) in a bowl and put in a safe spot. Add 6 eggs to a different bowl and beat with a hand blender until you get see rises at the top.
2. Soften the stick of margarine in the microwave and gradually add it to the eggs as you beat with the hand blender.
3. When wet and dry fixings are completely consolidated in isolated dishes, gradually add the dry fixings to the wet fixings as you blend in with the hand blender.
4. Oil an 8x4 portion dish and empty the blend into it equitably. Heat at 350 for 40-50 minutes (time will change contingent upon your broiler).
5. Let it rest for 10 minutes before expelling from the container. Cut up and appreciate it with spread or toasted!

Nutrition: 398

Calories: 21g

Fat: 4.7g

Carbs: 44.2g

Protein: 0 g

CHAPTER 14:

Gluten-Free Bread

126. Gluten-Free Simple Sandwich Bread

This bread is perfect for the gluten intolerant. It's a simple bread that travels, packs well, and tastes good. It is also suitable for the advanced bread maker as the instructions are explicit and detailed.

Preparation Time: 5 minutes

Cooking Time: 1 hour

Servings: 12

Ingredients:

- 1 1/2 cups sorghum flour
- 1 cup tapioca starch
- 1/2 cup gluten-free millet flour or gluten-free oat flour
- 2 teaspoons xanthan gum
- 1 1/4 teaspoons fine sea salt
- 2 1/2 teaspoons gluten-free yeast for bread machines
- 1 1/4 cups warm water
- 3 tablespoons extra virgin olive oil
- 1 tablespoon honey or raw agave nectar
- 1/2 tsp mild rice vinegar or lemon juice
- 2 organic eggs, beaten

Directions:

1. Mix the dry fixings except for the yeast and set aside.
2. Add the liquid ingredients to the bread maker pan first, then gently pour the mixed dry ingredients on top of the liquid.
3. Create a hole or well in the middle of the dry fixing and add the yeast. Set for Rapid 1 hour 20 minutes, medium crust color, and press Start.
4. Transfer to a cooling rack within 15 minutes before slicing to serve.

Nutrition:

Calories: 137 Fat: 4.6 g

Carbs: 22.1 g Protein: 2.4 g

127. Gluten-Free Chia Bread

This bread is excellent to eat with butter slathered all over it. It is great as breakfast, in the morning, with lunch or dinner.

Preparation Time: 5 minutes

Cooking Time: 3 hours

Servings: 12

Ingredients:

- 1 cup of warm water
- 3 large organic eggs, room temperature
- 1/4 cup olive oil
- 1 tablespoon apple cider vinegar
- 1 cup gluten-free chia seeds, ground to flour
- 1 cup almond meal flour
- 1/2 cup potato starch
- 1/4 cup coconut flour
- 3/4 cup millet flour
- 1 tablespoon xanthan gum
- 1 1/2 teaspoons salt
- 2 tablespoons sugar
- 3 tablespoons nonfat dry milk
- 6 teaspoons instant yeast

Directions:

1. Mix wet fixings and add to the bread maker pan. Whisk dry ingredients, except yeast, together and add on top of wet ingredients.
2. Make a well in the dry ingredients, add yeast, select Whole Wheat cycle, light crust color, and press Start. Allow cooling completely before serving.

Nutrition:

Calories: 375

Fat: 18.3 g

Carbs: 42 g

Protein: 12.2 g

128. Gluten-Free Brown Bread

This bread is excellent for toast, sandwiches, and as a breakfast bread.

Preparation Time: 5 minutes

Cooking Time: 3 hours

Servings: 12

Ingredients:

- 2 large eggs, lightly beaten
- 1 3/4 cups warm water
- 3 tablespoons canola oil

- 1 cup brown rice flour
- 3/4 cup oat flour
- 1/4 cup tapioca starch
- 1 1/4 cups potato starch
- 1 1/2 teaspoons salt
- 2 tablespoons brown sugar
- 2 tablespoons gluten-free flaxseed meal
- 1/2 cup nonfat dry milk powder
- 2 1/2 teaspoons xanthan gum
- 3 tablespoons psyllium, whole husks
- 2 1/2 teaspoons gluten-free yeast for bread machines

Directions:

1. Add the eggs, water, and canola oil to the bread maker pan and stir until combined. Whisk all of the dry ingredients except the yeast together in a large mixing bowl.
2. Put the dry fixings on top of the wet ingredients. Make a well in the center of the dry fixing and add the yeast.
3. Set to Gluten-Free cycle, medium crust color, and press Start. When the bread is done, lay the pan on its side to cool before slicing to serve.

Nutrition:

Calories: 201

Fat: 5.7 g

Carbs: 35.5 g

Protein: 5.1 g

129. Easy Gluten-Free, Dairy-Free Bread

This bread is a beautiful, delicious, and easy gluten-free, dairy-free bread. It can be eaten for breakfast, dinner, or dessert.

Preparation Time: 15 minutes

Cooking Time: 2 hours 10 minutes

Servings: 12

Ingredients:

- 1 1/2 cups warm water
- 2 teaspoons active dry yeast
- 2 teaspoons sugar
- 2 eggs, room temperature
- 1 egg white, room temperature
- 1 1/2 tablespoons apple cider vinegar
- 4 1/2 tablespoons olive oil
- 3 1/3 cups multi-purpose gluten-free flour

Directions:

1. Put the yeast plus sugar into the warm water and stir to mix in a large mixing bowl; set aside until foamy, about 8 to 10 minutes.

2. Whisk the 2 eggs and 1 egg white together in a separate mixing bowl and add to the bread maker's baking pan. Put apple cider vinegar plus oil in the baking pan.
3. Put foamy yeast/water batter into the baking pan. Add the multi-purpose gluten-free flour on top.
4. Set for Gluten-Free bread setting and Start. Remove and move onto a cooling rack, then allow to cool completely before slicing to serve.

Nutrition:

Calories: 241

Fat: 6.8 g

Carbs: 41 g

Protein: 4.5 g

130. Gluten-Free Sourdough Bread

This bread is made with a sourdough starter. Because the bread is "sour," it does not rise as high as non-sourdough gluten-free bread, but it is still delicious tasting and works well for sandwiches and toast. The bread is fairly dense and chewy.

Preparation Time: 5 minutes

Cooking Time: 3 hours

Servings: 12

Ingredients:

- 1 cup of water
- 3 eggs
- 3/4 cup ricotta cheese
- 1/4 cup honey
- 1/4 cup vegetable oil
- 1 teaspoon cider vinegar
- 3/4 cup gluten-free sourdough starter
- 2 cups white rice flour
- 2/3 cup potato starch
- 1/3 cup tapioca flour
- 1/2 cup dry milk powder
- 3 1/2 teaspoons xanthan gum
- 1 1/2 teaspoons salt

Directions:

1. Combine wet ingredients and pour into bread maker pan. Mix dry ingredients in a large mixing bowl, and add on top of the wet ingredients.
2. Select the Gluten-Free cycle and press Start. Remove the pan from the machine and allow the bread to remain in the pan for approximately 10 minutes. Transfer to a cooling rack before slicing.

Nutrition:

Calories: 299 Fat: 7.3 g

Carbs: 46 g

Protein: 5.2 g

131. Gluten-Free Crusty Boule Bread

This bread is packed with flavor, crusty on the outside and soft on the inside. Great for sandwiches and toast. No more frozen bread; instead of fresh from the bread machine, this bread is ready to slice and go.

Preparation Time: 15 minutes

Cooking Time: 3 hours

Servings: 12

Ingredients:

- 3 1/4 cups gluten-free flour mix
- 1 tablespoon active dry yeast
- 1 1/2 teaspoons kosher salt
- 1 tablespoon guar gum
- 1 1/3 cups warm water
- 2 large eggs, room temperature
- 2 tablespoons, plus 2 teaspoons olive oil
- 1 tablespoon honey

Directions:

1. Mix all of the dry fixings, except the yeast, in a large mixing bowl; set aside. Mix the water, eggs, oil, plus honey in a separate mixing bowl.
2. Pour the wet ingredients into the bread maker. Put the dry fixings on top of the wet ingredients.
3. Make a well in the center of the dry fixing and add the yeast. Set to Gluten-Free setting and press Start.
4. Remove baked bread and allow to cool completely. Hollow out and fill with soup or dip to use as a boule or slice for serving.

Nutrition:

Calories: 480 Fat: 3.2 g

Carbs: 103.9 g Protein: 2.4 g

132. Gluten-Free Potato Bread

This bread is quick and easy to make. It is so good, with jam or jelly.

Preparation Time: 5 minutes

Cooking Time: 3 hours

Servings: 12

Ingredients:

- 1 medium russet potato, baked, or mashed leftovers
- 2 packets gluten-free quick yeast

- 3 tablespoons honey
- 3/4 cup warm almond milk
- 2 eggs, 1 egg white
- 3 2/3 cups almond flour
- 3/4 cup tapioca flour
- 1 teaspoon of sea salt
- 1 teaspoon dried chives
- 1 tablespoon apple cider vinegar
- 1/4 cup olive oil

Directions:

1. Mix all of the dry fixings, except the yeast, in a large mixing bowl; set aside. Whisk together the milk, eggs, oil, apple cider, and honey in a separate mixing bowl.
2. Pour the wet ingredients into the bread maker. Add the dry ingredients on top of the wet ingredients.
3. Create a well in the dry fixings and add the yeast. Set to Gluten-Free bread setting, light crust color, and press Start. Allow cooling completely before slicing.

Nutrition:

Calories: 232

Fat: 13.2 g

Carbs: 17.4 g

Protein: 10.4 g

133. Gluten-Free Sorghum Bread Recipe

This bread is surprisingly good for gluten-free bread; it is very light and airy. Its crumb is very soft. It probably won't stand up to sandwich bread, but gluten-free people will love this bread. It makes a great sandwich loaf too.

Preparation Time: 5 minutes

Cooking Time: 3 hours

Servings: 12

Ingredients:

- 1 1/2 cups sorghum flour
- 1 cup tapioca starch
- 1/2 cup brown sweet rice flour
- 1 tsp xanthan gum
- 1 tsp guar gum
- 1/2 teaspoon salt
- 3 tablespoons sugar
- 2 1/4 teaspoons instant yeast
- 3 eggs (room temperature, lightly beaten)
- 1/4 cup oil
- 1 1/2 teaspoons vinegar
- 3/4-1 cup milk (105 - 115°F)

Directions:

1. Mix the dry fixings in a mixing bowl, except for the yeast. Put the wet

fixings in the bread maker pan, then add the dry ingredients on top.
2. Create a well or hole in the middle of the dry fixings and add the yeast. Set to Basic bread cycle, light crust color, and press Start. Remove and lay on its side to cool on a wire rack before serving.

Nutrition:

Calories: 169 Fat: 6.3 g

Carbs: 25.8 g

Protein: 3.3 g.

134. Gluten-Free Paleo Bread

This bread is about as close as you can get to the perfect gluten-free bread. When you cut a slice of this bread and hold it up to the light, you can see through it completely

Preparation Time: 10 minutes

Cooking Time: 3 hours 15 minutes

Servings: 16

Ingredients:

- 4 tablespoons chia seeds
- 1 tablespoon flax meal
- 3/4 cup, plus 1 tablespoon water
- 1/4 cup coconut oil
- 3 eggs, room temperature
- 1/2 cup almond milk
- 1 tablespoon honey
- 2 cups almond flour
- 1 1/4 cups tapioca flour
- 1/3 cup coconut flour
- 1 teaspoon salt
- 1/4 cup flax meal
- 2 teaspoons cream of tartar
- 1 teaspoon baking soda
- 2 teaspoons active dry yeast

Directions:

1. Mix the chia seeds plus 1 tablespoon of flax meal in a mixing bowl; stir in the water and set aside. Dissolve coconut oil in a microwave-safe dish, and let it cool down to lukewarm.
2. Whisk in the eggs, almond milk, and honey. Whisk in the chia seeds and flax meal gel and pour it into the bread maker pan.
3. Mix the almond flour, tapioca flour, coconut flour, salt, and 1/4 cup of flax meal. Mix the cream of tartar plus baking soda in a separate bowl and combine it with the other dry ingredients.
4. Pour the dry ingredients into the bread machine. Make a little well on top and add the yeast. Start the machine on the Wheat cycle, light or medium crust color, and press Start.

5. Remove to cool completely before slicing to serve.

Nutrition: Calories: 190 Fat: 10.3 g

Carbs: 20.4 g Protein: 4.5 g

135. Gluten-Free Oat & Honey Bread

This bread is easy to make and keeps well for up to a week when stored in an air-tight container.

Preparation Time: 5 minutes

Cooking Time: 3 hours

Servings: 12

Ingredients:

- 1 1/4 cups warm water
- 3 tablespoons honey
- 2 eggs
- 3 tablespoons butter, melted
- 1 1/4 cups gluten-free oats
- 1 1/4 cups brown rice flour
- 1/2 cup potato starch
- 2 teaspoons xanthan gum
- 1 1/2 teaspoons sugar
- 3/4 teaspoon salt
- 1 1/2 tablespoons active dry yeast

Directions:

1. Add ingredients in the order listed above, except for the yeast. Make a well in the center of the dry fixings and add the yeast.
2. Select a Gluten-Free cycle, light crust color, and press Start. Remove bread and allow the bread to cool on its side on a cooling rack for 20 minutes before slicing to serve.

Nutrition: Calories: 151 Fat: 4.5 g

Carbs: 27.2 g Protein: 3.5 g

136. Gluten-Free Cinnamon Raisin Bread

This bread is tasty and moist. It can excellently be made in a bread machine.

Preparation Time: 5 minutes

Cooking Time: 3 hours

Servings: 12

Ingredients:

- 3/4 cup almond milk

- 2 tablespoons flax meal
- 6 tablespoons warm water
- 1 1/2 teaspoons apple cider vinegar
- 2 tablespoons butter
- 1 1/2 tablespoons honey
- 1 2/3 cups brown rice flour
- 1/4 cup corn starch
- 2 tablespoons potato starch
- 1 1/2 teaspoons xanthan gum
- 1 tablespoon cinnamon
- 1/2 teaspoon salt
- 1 teaspoon active dry yeast
- 1/2 cup raisins

Directions:

1. Mix flax plus water and let stand for 5 minutes. Combine dry ingredients in a separate bowl, except for the yeast.
2. Add wet ingredients to the bread machine. Add the dry mixture on top and make a well in the middle of the dry mix. Add the yeast to the well.
3. Set to Gluten-Free, light crust color, and press Start. After the first kneading and rise cycle, add raisins. Remove to a cooling rack when baked and let cool for 15 minutes before slicing.

Nutrition:

Calories: 192

Fat: 4.7 g

Carbs: 38.2 g

Protein: 2.7 g

137. Gluten-Free Pumpkin Pie Bread

This bread is so moist and can help make your holiday meals easier.

Preparation Time: 5 minutes

Cooking Time: 2 hours 50 minutes

Servings: 12

Ingredients:

- 1/4 cup olive oil
- 2 large eggs, beaten
- 1 tablespoon bourbon vanilla extract
- 1 cup canned pumpkin
- 4 tablespoons honey
- 1/4 teaspoon lemon juice
- 1/2 cup buckwheat flour
- 1/4 cup millet flour
- 1/4 cup sorghum flour
- 1/2 cup tapioca starch
- 1 cup light brown sugar
- 2 teaspoons baking powder
- 1 teaspoon baking soda
- 1/2 teaspoon sea salt
- 1 teaspoon xanthan gum
- 1 teaspoon ground cinnamon
- 1 teaspoon allspice

- 1-2 tablespoons peach juice

Directions:

1. Mix dry fixings in a bowl and put aside. Add wet ingredients to the pan, except peach juice. Add mixed dry ingredients to the bread maker pan.
2. Set to Sweet bread cycle, light or medium crust color, and press Start. As it begins to mix the ingredients, use a soft silicone spatula to scrape down the sides.
3. If the batter is stiff, add one tablespoon at a peach juice time until the batter becomes slightly thinner than muffin batter.
4. Close the lid and allow to bake. Remove to a cooling rack within 20 minutes before slicing.

Nutrition:

Calories: 180 Fat: 5.5 g

Carbs: 33.1 g Protein: 2.4 g

138. Gluten-Free Pizza Crust

Gluten-Free Pizza Crust is reminiscent of fresh bread dough, soft, with a nice crispy crust.

Preparation Time: 10 minutes

Cooking Time: 2 hours

Servings: 6 – 8

Ingredients:

- 3 large eggs, room temperature
- 1/2 cup olive oil
- 1 cup milk
- 1/2 cup water
- 2 cups of rice flour
- 1 cup cornstarch, and extra for dusting
- 1/2 cup potato starch
- 1/2 cup sugar
- 2 tablespoons yeast
- 3 teaspoons xanthan gum
- 1 teaspoon salt

Directions:

1. Mix the wet fixings in a separate bowl and pour into the bread maker pan. Combine the dry fixings except for the yeast and add to the pan.
2. Create a well or a hole in the middle of the dry fixings and add the yeast, then select Dough cycle and press Start.
3. When the dough is finished, press it out on a surface lightly sprinkled with corn starch and create a pizza shape. Use this dough with your favorite toppings and pizza recipe!

Nutrition:

Calories: 463 Fat: 15.8 g

Carbs: 79.2 g

Protein: 7.4 g

139. Gluten-Free Whole Grain Bread

This bread is high in protein, has lots of fiber.

Preparation Time: 15 minutes

Cooking Time: 3 hours 40 minutes

Servings: 12

Ingredients:

- 2/3 cup sorghum flour
- 1/2 cup buckwheat flour
- 1/2 cup millet flour
- 3/4 cup potato starch
- 2 1/4 teaspoons xanthan gum
- 1 1/4 teaspoons salt
- 3/4 cup skim milk
- 1/2 cup water
- 1 tablespoon instant yeast
- 5 teaspoons agave nectar, separated
- 1 large egg, lightly beaten
- 4 tablespoons extra virgin olive oil
- 1/2 teaspoon cider vinegar
- 1 tablespoon poppy seeds

Directions:

1. Whisk sorghum, buckwheat, millet, potato starch, xanthan gum, and sea salt in a bowl and set aside.
2. Combine milk and water in a glass measuring cup. Heat to between 110°F and 120°F; add 2 teaspoons of agave nectar and yeast and stir to combine. Cover and set aside for a few minutes.
3. Combine the egg, olive oil, remaining agave, and vinegar in another mixing bowl; add yeast and milk mixture. Pour wet ingredients into the bottom of your bread maker.
4. Top with dry ingredients. Select a Gluten-Free cycle, light color crust, and press Start after second kneading cycle, sprinkle with poppy seeds.
5. Remove pan from the bread machine. Leave the loaf in the pan for about 5 minutes before cooling on a rack. Enjoy!

Nutrition:

Calories: 153

Fat: 5.9 g

Carbs: 24.5 g

Protein: 3.3 g

140. Gluten-Free Pull-Apart Rolls

Gluten-Free Pull-Apart Rolls is a stunning recipe that has been tried and tested for taste. This recipe is perfect for serving the whole family, as your children will adore the mixture of flavor and texture provided by the various ingredients.

Preparation Time: 5 minutes

Cooking Time: 2 hours

Servings: 9

Ingredients:

- 1 cup of warm water
- 2 tablespoons butter, unsalted
- 1 egg, room temperature
- 1 teaspoon apple cider vinegar
- 2 3/4 cups gluten-free almond-blend flour
- 1 1/2 teaspoons xanthan gum
- 1/4 cup sugar
- 1 teaspoon salt
- 2 teaspoons active dry yeast

Directions:

1. Add wet ingredients to the bread maker pan. Mix dry ingredients except for yeast, and put in a pan. Make a well in the center of the dry ingredients and add the yeast.
2. Select the Dough cycle and press Start. Spray an 8-inch round cake pan with non-stick cooking spray.
3. When it's done, roll the dough out into 9 balls, place in a cake pan, and baste each with warm water.
4. Wrap using a towel and let rise in a warm place for 1 hour—Preheat oven to 400°F. Bake for 26 to 28 minutes; until golden brown. Brush with butter and serve.

Nutrition:

Calories: 568

Fat: 10.5 g

Carbs: 116.3 g

Protein: 8.6 g

CHAPTER 15:

Breakfast, Fruit and Chocolate Bread

141. English Muffin Bread

English Muffin Bread is the best bread known to the Haidan Sector.

The bread has a texture similar to the muffins used on Earth that have made them so popular.

This bread is made by everything that uses readily available items and is fairly easy to make.

Preparation time: 5 minutes

Cooking time: 3 hours 40 minutes

Servings: 14

Ingredients:

- 1 teaspoon vinegar
- 1/4 to 1/3 cup water
- 1 cup lukewarm milk
- 2 tablespoon butter or 2 tablespoon vegetable oil
- 1½ teaspoon salt
- 1½ teaspoon sugar
- ½ teaspoon baking powder
- 3½ cups unbleached all-purpose flour
- 2 1/4 teaspoon instant yeast

Directions:

1. Add each ingredient to the bread machine in the order and at the temperature recommended by your bread machine manufacturer.
2. Close the lid, select the basic bread, low crust setting on your bread machine, and press start.
3. When the bread machine has finished baking, remove the bread and put it on a cooling rack.

Nutrition:

Calories: 62

Carbs: 13g

Fat: 1g

Protein: 2g

142. Cranberry Orange Breakfast Bread

Cranberry Orange Breakfast Bread is like having cranberry orange muffins baked in the bread machine.

Preparation time: 5 minutes

Cooking time: 3 hours 10 minutes

Servings: 14

Ingredients:

- 1 1/8 cup orange juice
- 2 tablespoon vegetable oil
- 2 tablespoon honey
- 3 cups bread flour
- 1 tablespoon dry milk powder
- ½ teaspoon ground cinnamon
- ½ teaspoon ground allspice
- 1 teaspoon salt
- 1 (.25 ounce) package active dry yeast
- 1 tablespoon grated orange zest
- 1 cup sweetened dried cranberries
- 1/3 cup chopped walnuts.

Directions:

1. Add each ingredient to the bread machine in the order and at the temperature recommended by your bread machine manufacturer.
2. Close the lid, select the basic bread, low crust setting on your bread machine, and press start. Add the cranberries and chopped walnuts 5 to 10 minutes before the last kneading cycle ends.
3. When the bread machine has finished baking, remove the bread and put it on a cooling rack.

Nutrition: Calories: 56 Carbs: 29g

Fat: 2g Protein: 9g

143. Buttermilk Honey Bread

This bread is very light and slightly sweet. It's great for morning toast!

Preparation time: 5 minutes

Cooking time: 3 hours 45 minutes

Servings: 14

Ingredients:

- ½ cup of water
- ¾ cup buttermilk

- ¼ cup honey
- 3 tablespoon butter, softened and cut into pieces
- 3 cups bread flour
- 1½ teaspoon salt
- 2¼ teaspoon yeast (or 1 package)

Directions:

1. Add each ingredient to the bread machine in the order and at the temperature recommended by your bread machine manufacturer.
2. Close the lid, select the basic bread, medium crust setting on your bread machine, and press start. When the bread machine has finished baking, remove the bread and put it on a cooling rack.

Nutrition: Calories: 92 Carbs: 19g

Fat: 1g Protein: 2g

144. Whole Wheat Breakfast Bread

This bread is as soft and delicious as any white bread you can buy, and whole wheat, too. It's an easy bread to make and a good one to start with when you are first learning to use a bread machine.

Preparation time: 5 minutes

Cooking time: 3 hours 45 minutes

Servings: 14

Ingredients:

- 3 cups white whole wheat flour
- ½ teaspoon salt
- 1 cup of water
- ½ cup coconut oil, liquefied
- 4 tablespoon honey
- 2½ teaspoon active dry yeast

Directions:

1. Add each ingredient to the bread machine in the order and at the temperature recommended by your bread machine manufacturer.
2. Close the lid, select the basic bread, medium crust setting on your bread machine, and press start. When the bread machine has finished baking, remove the bread and put it on a cooling rack.

Nutrition:

Calories: 60

Carbs: 11g

Fat: 3g

Protein: 1g

145. Cinnamon-Raisin Bread

The chunks of golden raisins stuffed inside and cinnamon are a real hit to anyone who eats this.

Preparation time: 5 minutes

Cooking time: 3 hours

Servings: 4

Ingredients:

- 1 cup of water
- 2 tablespoon butter, softened
- 3 cups Gold Medal Better for Bread flour
- 3 tablespoon sugar
- 1½ teaspoon salt
- 1 teaspoon ground cinnamon
- 2½ teaspoon bread machine yeast
- ¾ cup raisins

Directions:

1. Add the ingredient except for the raisins to the bread machine.
2. Close the lid, select the sweet or basic bread, medium crust setting on your bread machine, and press start. Add raisins 10 minutes before the last kneading cycle ends.
3. When the bread machine has finished baking, remove the bread and put it on a cooling rack.

Nutrition:

Calories: 180

Carbs: 38g

Fat: 2g

Protein: 4g

146. Butter Bread Rolls

This bread is an easy recipe to fix. Sometimes it is nice to make rolls to go along with other meals.

Preparation time: 50 minutes

Cooking time: 45 minutes

Servings: 24 rolls

Ingredients:

- 1 cup warm milk
- 1/2 cup butter or 1/2 cup margarine, softened
- 1/4 cup sugar

- 2 eggs
- 1 1/2 teaspoons salt
- 4 cups bread flour
- 2 1/4 teaspoons active dry yeast

Directions:

1. In the bread machine pan, put all ingredients in the order suggested by the manufacturer. Select dough setting. When the cycle is completed, turn dough onto a lightly floured surface.
2. Divide dough into 24 portions. Shape dough into balls. Place in a greased 13 inch by the 9-inch baking pan.
3. Wrap the dough, then allow to rise in a warm area for 30-45 minutes. Bake at 350 degrees for 13-16 minutes or until golden brown.

Nutrition:

Calories: 180 Carbs: 38g

Fat: 2g

Protein: 4g

147. Cranberry & Golden Raisin Bread

This bread is great to have on hand when there are unexpected guests at your house so that they can take some home with them.

Preparation time: 5 minutes

Cooking time: 3 hours

Servings: 14

Ingredients:

- 1 1/3 cups water
- 4 tablespoon sliced butter
- 3 cups flour
- 1 cup old fashioned oatmeal
- 1/3 cup brown sugar
- 1 teaspoon salt
- 4 tablespoon dried cranberries
- 4 tablespoon golden raisins
- 2 teaspoon bread machine yeast

Directions:

1. According to the manufacturer's instructions, add each ingredient except cranberries and golden raisins to the bread machine one by one.
2. Close the lid, select the sweet or basic bread, medium crust setting on your bread machine, and press start.
3. Add the cranberries and golden raisins 5 to 10 minutes before the last kneading cycle ends. When the bread machine has finished baking, remove the bread and put it on a cooling rack.

Nutrition:

Calories: 175 Carbs: 33g

Fat: 3g

Protein: 4g

148. Chocolate Cherry Bread

This bread is excellent. It is perfect to use up cherries for anyone who puts up fruit preserves. It makes a soft, springy loaf, which will bake in a 3-pound size bread machine.

Preparation time: 5 minutes

Cooking time: 3 hours

Servings: 14 slices

Ingredients:

- 1 cup milk
- 1 egg
- 3 Tbsp water
- 4 tsp butter
- ½ tsp almond extract
- 4 cups bread flour
- 3 tbsp sugar
- 1 tsp salt
- 1¼ tsp active dry yeast
- ½ cup dried cherries snipped
- ½ cup semisweet chocolate pieces, chilled

Directions:

1. Add each ingredient to the bread machine in the order and at the temperature recommended by your bread machine manufacturer.
2. Close the lid, select the sweet loaf, low crust setting on your bread machine, and press start. When the bread machine has finished baking, remove the bread, and put it on a cooling rack.

Nutrition:

Calories 210 Carbs 23 g

Fat 13 g Protein 3 g

149. Chocolate Orange Bread

This bread is very moist plus has a great orange flavor. It's very thin, so it's suitable for toast or bread pudding.

Preparation time: 10 minutes

Cooking time: 3 hours & 10 minutes

Servings: 14 slices

Ingredients:

- 1 5/8 cups strong white bread flour
- 2 tbsp cocoa
- 1 tsp ground mixed spice
- 1 egg, beaten
- ½ cup of water
- ¼ cup of orange juice

- 2 tbsp butter
- 3 tbsp light muscovado sugar
- 1 tsp salt
- 1½ tsp easy bake yeast
- ¾ cup mixed peel
- ¾ cup of chocolate chips

Directions:

1. Sift the flour, cocoa, and spices together in a bowl. Add each ingredient to the bread machine in the order and at the temperature recommended by your bread machine manufacturer.
2. Close the lid, select the sweet loaf, medium crust setting on your bread machine, and press start. Add the mixed peel and chocolate chips 5 to 10 minutes before the last kneading cycle ends.
3. When the bread machine has finished baking, remove the bread and put it on a cooling rack.

Nutrition:

Calories 197

Carbs 35 g

Fat 6 g

Protein 2 g

150. Almond Chocolate Chip Bread

This bread is a wonderfully rich dessert bread and will keep for days. Use it whenever a chocolate dessert is called for or for breakfast.

Preparation time: 10 minutes

Cooking time: 3 hours

Servings: 14 slices

Ingredients:

- 1 cup plus 2 tbsp water
- 2 tbsp softened butter
- ½ tsp vanilla
- 3 cups Gold Medal Better for Bread flour
- ¾ cup semisweet chocolate chips
- 3 tbsp sugar
- 1 tbsp dry milk
- ¾ tsp salt
- 1½ tsp quick active dry yeast
- 1/3 cup sliced almonds

Directions:

1. Add all fixings except the almonds to the bread machine. Close the lid,

select the sweet loaf, low crust setting on your bread machine, and press start.
2. Add almonds 10 minutes before the last kneading cycle ends. When the bread machine has finished baking, remove the bread and put it on a cooling rack.

Nutrition: Calories 225 Carbs 37 g

Fat 7 g Protein 5 g

151. Walnut Cocoa Bread

This bread is fabulously adaptable and very easy.

Preparation time: 10 minutes

Cooking time: 3 hours

Servings: 14 slices

Ingredients:

- 2/3 cup milk
- 1/3 cup water
- 5 tbsp butter, softened
- 1/3 cup packed brown sugar
- 5 tbsp baking cocoa
- 1 tsp salt
- 3 cups bread flour
- 2¼ tsp active dry yeast
- 2/3 cup chopped walnuts, toasted

Directions:
1. Add each ingredient except the walnuts to the bread machine.
2. Close the lid, select the sweet loaf, low crust setting on your bread machine, and press start. Just before the final kneading, add the walnuts.
3. When the bread machine has finished baking, remove the bread and put it on a cooling rack.

Nutrition: Calories 168 Carbs 23 g

Fat 7 g Protein 5 g

152. Mexican Chocolate Bread

This bread is as easy to make in the bread machine as you may think. It bakes up beautifully. It's also a quick bread. So, you can have it ready to eat anytime.

Preparation time: 10 minutes

Cooking time: 3 hours & 10 minutes

Servings: 14 slices

Ingredients:

- ½ cup milk

- ½ cup of orange juice
- 1 large egg plus 1 egg yolk
- 3 tbsp unsalted butter cut into pieces
- 2½ cups bread flour
- ¼ cup light brown sugar
- 3 tbsp unsweetened Dutch-process cocoa powder - 1 tbsp gluten
- 1 tsp instant espresso powder
- ¾ tsp ground cinnamon
- ½ cup bittersweet chocolate chips
- 2½ tsp bread machine yeast

Directions:

1. Add each ingredient to the bread machine in the order and at the temperature recommended by your bread machine manufacturer.
2. Close the lid, select the sweet loaf, low crust setting on your bread machine, and press start. When the bread machine has finished baking, remove the bread and put it on a cooling rack.

Nutrition: Calories 250 Carbs 32 g

Fat 9 g Protein 5 g

153. Banana Chocolate Chip Bread

This bread is moist and delicious. The addition of chocolate chips makes this an extra special treat.

Preparation time: 10 minutes

Cooking time: 2 hours

Servings: 14 slices

Ingredients:

- 2 eggs
- 1/3 cup melted butter
- 1/8 cup milk
- 2 mashed bananas
- 2 cups all-purpose bread flour
- 2/3 cup sugar
- 1¼ tsp baking powder
- ½ tsp baking soda
- ½ tsp salt
- ½ cup chopped walnuts
- ½ cup of chocolate chips

Directions:

1. Add each ingredient to the bread machine in the order and at the temperature recommended by your bread machine manufacturer.
2. Close the lid, select the quick bread, low crust setting on your bread machine, and press start. When the bread machine has finished baking, remove the bread and put it on a cooling rack.

Nutrition:

Calories 262

Carbs 36 g

Fat 11 g

Protein 4 g

154. Chocolate Chip Bread

This bread is something of a treat for a brunch or a special occasion like Christmas. The chocolate chips are a festive touch, but you can use raisins or dried cranberries for a fruitier version. The bread machine makes it easy to mix and bake.

Preparation time: 5 minutes

Cooking time: 3 hours

Servings: 14 slices

Ingredients:

- ¼ cup of water - 1 cup milk
- 1 egg - 3 cups bread flour
- 3 tbsp brown sugar
- 2 tbsp white sugar
- 1 tsp salt
- 1 tsp ground cinnamon
- 1½ tsp active dry yeast
- 2 tbsp margarine, softened
- ¾ cup semisweet chocolate chips

Directions:

1. Add each ingredient except the chocolate chips to the bread machine in the order and at the temperature recommended by your bread machine manufacturer.
2. Close the lid, select the sweet loaf, low crust setting on your bread machine, and press start. Add the chocolate chips about 5 minutes before the kneading cycle has finished. When the bread machine has finished baking, remove the bread and put it on a cooling rack.

Nutrition: Calories 184 Carbs 20 g

Fat 5 g Protein 5 g

155. Sunny Delight Loaf

This bread is made in a bread machine, so you have no last-minute preparation work. A family of four can easily eat it all and freeze any leftovers for toast or sandwiches.

Preparation time: 20 minutes

Cooking time: 3 hours

Servings: 12 slices

Ingredients

For the Bread:

- 3 1/2 cups all-purpose flour

- ¾ cup sweet almonds, chopped
- 3 tbsp brown sugar
- 2 tbsp freshly grated orange zest
- 1 cup orange juice
- 2 tbsp sweet almond oil
- 1 tsp salt
- 1 tsp vanilla extract
- 2 tsp bread machine yeast

For the glaze:

- 1 ½ tbsp Sweet almonds, chopped
- 3 tbsp orange jam

Directions:

1. Put all fixings to your bread machine, carefully following the instructions of the manufacturer.
2. Set the bread machine program to Basic/White Bread and set crust type to Medium, and press START. Wait until the cycle completes.
3. Once the loaf is ready, take the bucket out and let the loaf cool within 5 minutes. Shake the bucket to remove the loaf.
4. Spread the jam and almonds on the top of the loaf. Transfer to a cooling rack, slice, and serve. Enjoy!

Nutrition:

Calories: 347

Carbs: 61g

Fat: 7g

Protein: 8g

156. Dark Rye Loaf

This bread is excellent for making a holiday bread.

Preparation time: 20 minutes

Cooking time: 3 hours & 10 minutes

Servings: 12 slices

Ingredients

- 300 ml water 80°f (27°c)
- 1 tbsp melted butter, at room temperature
- 2 tbsp molasses
- 1 tsp salt
- 1 tbsp unsweetened cocoa powder
- 3 tbsp brown sugar
- 1 ½ cup rye flour
- caraway seed (optional)
- 2 cups all-purpose flour
- 2 tsp bread machine yeast

Directions:

1. Add all ingredients to your bread machine, carefully following the instructions of the manufacturer.

Make a groove in the flour and add yeast.
2. Set your bread machine program to Basic/White Bread and set crust type to Medium, and press Start. Wait until the cycle completes.
3. Once the loaf is ready, take the bucket out and let the loaf cool within 5 minutes. Shake the bucket to remove the loaf. Slice, and serve. Enjoy!

Nutrition:

Calories: 159

Carbs: 32g

Fat: 2g

Protein: 4g

157. Paradise Bread

This bread is a classic Hawaiian breakfast bread. Called Paradise bread, it is known for its rather strange looking top. Enjoy the bread with a tropical fruit spread.

Preparation time: 10 minutes

Cooking time: 3 hours

Servings: 12 slices

Ingredients:

- 3 cups bread flour
- 1 large egg, at room temperature
- ¾ cup pineapple juice
- 37 ml honey
- 2 tbsp vegetable oil
- 2 tbsp dry milk
- 2 tsp fast rising yeast
- ¾ tsp salt

Directions:

1. Put all fixings to your bread machine, carefully following the instructions of the manufacturer. Make a groove in the flour and add yeast.
2. Set your bread machine program to Basic/White Bread and set crust type to Medium, and press Start. Wait until the cycle completes.
3. Once the loaf is ready, take the bucket out and let the loaf cool within 5 minutes. Shake the bucket to remove the loaf. Slice, and serve.

Nutrition:

Calories: 170

Carbs: 30g

Fat: 4g

Protein: 5g

158. Bran Packed Healthy Bread

This bread is packed with Bran. It is low glycemic and more nutritious than other types of bread.

Preparation time: 10 minutes

Cooking time: 2 hours

Servings: 8 slices

Ingredients:

- ¾ cup milk
- 1½ tbsp melted butter, at room temperature
- 1 tbsp sugar
- 1 tsp salt
- ½ cup wheat bran
- 2 cups white bread flour
- 1 tsp instant yeast

Directions:

1. Add all of the fixings to your bread machine, carefully following the instructions of the manufacturer.
2. Set the program of your bread machine to Basic/White Bread and set crust type to light. Press Start. Wait until the cycle completes.
3. Once the loaf is ready, take the bucket out and let the loaf cool within 5 minutes. Shake the bucket to remove the loaf. Slice, and serve.

Nutrition:

Calories: 198

Carbs: 34g

Fat: 6g

Protein: 4g

159. Orange Walnut Candied Loaf

This bread is excellent for breakfast or dessert. It's a light, tender sponge studded with walnuts and orange.

Preparation time: 10 minutes

Cooking time: 1 hour 30 minutes

Servings: 12 slices

Ingredients:

- 1/2 cup warm whey
- 1 tbsp bread machine yeast
- 4 tbsp sugar
- 1/2 cup orange juice
- 3 2/3 cups all-purpose flour
- 1 tsp salt
- 3 tsp orange zest
- 1/3 tsp vanilla
- 1/3 cup walnut + almonds
- ½ cup candied fruit

Directions:

1. Add all of the fixings to your bread machine, carefully following the instructions of the manufacturer.
2. Set the program of your bread machine to Cake setting and press Start. Once ready, take the bread and let it cool for 20 minutes. Slice and serve.

Nutrition: Calories: 437 Carbs: 82g

Fat: 7g Protein: 12g

160. Orchard's Dream Bread

Orchard's Dream Bread is a white bread machine bread. It is an all-purpose white bread — perfect for sandwiches, toast, and as the base of French toast.

Preparation time: 15 minutes

Cooking time: 3 hours

Servings: 12 slices

Ingredients:

- 1 cup lukewarm water
- 2 tbsp butter, softened
- 3 cups all-purpose flour
- ¼ cup brown sugar
- 2 tsp ground cinnamon
- 1 tsp salt
- 2 tsp active dry yeast
- 2/3 cup apple, chopped peeled
- 1/3 cup coarsely chopped pecans, toasted

Directions:

1. Add all of the fixings to your bread machine (except apples and pecans), carefully following the manufacturer's instructions.
2. Put the apples and pecans in the fruit and nut dispenser. If you lack a fruit and nut dispenser, you can add nuts directly to the bread pan when you hear the added ingredient beep.
3. Set the program of your bread machine to Basic/White Bread and set crust type to Medium. Press Start.
4. Once the loaf is ready, take the bucket out and let the loaf cool within 5 minutes. Shake the bucket to remove the loaf. Slice, and serve.

Nutrition: Calories: 185 Carbs: 32g

Fat: 5g Protein: 4g

161. Sesame Seeds & Onion Bread

Sesame Seeds & Onion Bread is a simple, flavorful bread made with a Bread Machine or scratch.

Preparation time: 10 minutes

Cooking time: 3 hours

Servings: 10 slices

Ingredients:

- ¾ cup lukewarm water
- 3 2/3 cups all-purpose flour
- ¾ cup cottage cheese

- 2 tbsp butter, softened
- 2 tbsp sugar
- 1½ tsp salt
- 1½ tbsp sesame seeds
- 2 tbsp dried onion
- 1¼ tsp dry yeast

Directions:

1. Put all fixings to your bread machine, carefully following the instructions of the manufacturer.
2. Set the program of your bread machine to Basic/White Bread and set crust type to Medium. Press Start.
3. Once the loaf is ready, take the bucket out, and let the loaf cool within 5 minutes. Shake the bucket to remove the loaf. Slice, and serve.

Nutrition: Calories: 277 Carbs: 48g

Fat: 5g Protein: 10g

162. Multigrain Bread with Honey

Multigrain Bread with Honey is phenomenal both for its aroma and its taste.

Preparation time: 10 minutes

Cooking time: 2 hours

Servings: 8 slices

Ingredients:

- ¾ cup lukewarm water
- 1 tbsp butter, softened
- ½ tbsp honey
- ½ tsp salt
- ¾ cup multigrain flour
- 1/3 cups wheat flour
- 1 tsp active dry yeast

Directions:

1. Put all fixings to your bread machine, carefully following the instructions of the manufacturer.
2. Set the program of your bread machine to Basic/White Bread and set crust type to Medium. Press Start. Once the loaf is ready, take the bucket out and let the loaf cool within 5 minutes.
3. Shake the bucket to remove the loaf. Slice, and serve.

Nutrition:

Calories: 145

Carbs: 27g

Fat: 2g

Protein: 4g

163. Rice Bread

Rice Bread is made in the bread machine. It is nutritious, of Indian origin, can serve as a sandwich bread (cut into squares), and is a favorite of kids.

Preparation time: 10 minutes

Cooking time: 3 hours

Servings: 16 slices

Ingredients:

- 4 ½ cups wheat flour
- 1 cup of rice cooked
- 1 large egg, at room temperature
- 2 tbsp dry milk
- 2 tsp bread machine yeast
- 2 tbsp butter, softened
- 1 tbsp sugar
- 1 ½ tsp salt
- 1 ¼ cups lukewarm water

Directions:

1. Put all fixings into your bread machine, carefully following the instructions of the manufacturer.
2. Set the program of your bread machine to Basic/White Bread and set crust type to Medium. Press Start.
3. Once the loaf is ready, remove the bucket and let the loaf cool for 5 minutes. Gently shake or wiggle the bucket to remove the loaf. Slice, and serve.

Nutrition:

Calories: 328

Carbs: 61g

Fat: 5g

Protein: 9g

164. Crunchy Wheat Herbed Bread

Crunchy Wheat Herbed Bread is a thin crust bread that makes healthy snacking and meal-partner. Although it does not go stale quickly, it tastes best if eaten within 24 hours of baking.

Preparation time: 30 minutes

Cooking time: 3 hours 40 minutes

Servings: 12 slices

Ingredients:

- 1¼ cups lukewarm water
- 1½ cups bread flour
- 1½ cups whole wheat flour
- 2 tbsp sugar
- 2 tbsp dry milk
- 2 tbsp butter, softened
- 1½ tsp salt

- 1½ tsp dried basil leaves
- 1 tsp dried thyme leaves
- 2 tsp bread machine yeast
- ½ cup sunflower nuts, toasted

Directions:

1. Add all the fixings to your bread machine, carefully following the manufacturer's instructions (except nuts).
2. Put the nuts in the fruit and nut dispenser. If you don't have a fruit and nut dispenser, you can add nuts directly to the bread pan when you hear the added ingredient beep.
3. Set your bread machine program to Basic/White Bread and set crust type to Medium or Light. Press Start.
4. Once the loaf is ready, take the bucket out, and let the loaf cool within 5 minutes. Shake the bucket to remove the loaf. Slice, and serve.

Nutrition: Calories: 170 Carbs: 28g

Fat: 5g Protein: 6g

165. Flower Power Bread

Flower Power Bread is very healthy bread. It uses no sugar, oil, or fat.

Preparation time: 10 minutes

Cooking time: 3 hours

Servings: 12 slices

Ingredients:

- 1 cup+ 1 tbsp water 160°f (70°c)
- ¼ cup honey
- 2 tbsp butter, softened
- 3 cups bread flour
- ½ cup quick-cooking oats
- 2 tbsp dry milk
- 1¼ tsp salt
- 2¼ tsp bread machine yeast
- ½ cup sunflower nuts, toasted

Directions:

1. Add all of the fixings to your bread machine, carefully following the manufacturer's instructions (except sunflower nuts).
2. Set the program of your bread machine to Basic/White Bread and set crust type to light. Press Start.
3. Once the machine beeps, add sunflower nuts (check dough after 5 minutes of mixing; add 1 to 2 tablespoons of water or flour if needed).
4. Once the loaf is ready, take the bucket out, and let the loaf cool for 5 minutes. Gently wiggle or shake the bucket to remove the loaf. Slice, and serve.

Nutrition:

Calories: 144 Carbs: 24g

Fat: 5g Protein: 5g

CHAPTER 16:

International Bread, Pizza and Focaccia

166. German Pumpernickel Bread

This bread is well suited to be sliced thinly and put into a breadbox.

It will keep for several weeks if it is well wrapped and moistened and will need no further toasting.

It is a bread well suited for the midnight craving.

Preparation time: 2 hours

Cooking time: 1 hour and 10 minutes

Servings: 1 loaf

Ingredients:

- 1 1/2 tablespoon vegetable oil
- 1 1/8 cups warm water
- 3 tablespoons cocoa
- 1/3 cup molasses
- 1 ½ teaspoons salt
- 1 tablespoon caraway seed
- 1 cup rye flour
- 1 ½ cups of bread flour
- 1 ½ tablespoon wheat gluten
- 1 cup whole wheat flour
- 2 ½ teaspoons bread machine yeast

Directions:

1. Put everything in your bread machine.
2. Select the primary cycle. Hit the start button.
3. Transfer bread to a rack for cooling once done.

Nutrition:

Calories 119

Carbohydrates: 22.4 g

Fat 2.3 g

Protein 3 g

167. European Black Bread

This bread is well known to people in Northern Europe; particularly, in the Nordic countries. The German name for the bread is "Schwarzbrot" (Black Bread), and it is very much a national bread of Sweden. It makes a delicious base for sandwiches and can make a variety of sweet and savory treats.

Preparation time: 2 hours

Cooking time: 1 hour and 5 minutes

Servings: 1 loaf

Ingredients:

- ¾ teaspoon cider vinegar
- 1 cup of water
- ½ cup rye flour
- 1 ½ cups flour
- 1 tablespoon margarine
- ¼ cup of oat bran
- 1 teaspoon salt
- 1 ½ tablespoons sugar
- 1 teaspoon dried onion flakes
- 1 teaspoon caraway seed
- 1 teaspoon yeast
- 2 tablespoons unsweetened cocoa

Directions:

1. Put everything in your bread machine. Now select the basic setting. Hit the start button. Transfer bread to a rack for cooling once done.

Nutrition:

Calories 114

Carbohydrates: 22 g

Fat 1.7 g

Protein 3 g

168. French Baguettes

This bread is nothing like the baguettes you get in the stores. It has none of the lop-sidedness of chain store bread. It has a crust that breaks sharply when you take a bite, as it was designed to do. It is crisp on the outside and chewy on the inside.

Preparation time: 25 minutes

Cooking time: 15 minutes

Servings: 2 loaves

Ingredients:

- 1 ¼ cups warm water
- 3 ½ cups bread flour
- 1 teaspoon salt
- 1 package active dry yeast

Directions:

1. Place ingredients in the bread machine. Select the dough cycle. Hit the start button. When it's done, remove it with floured hands and cut it in half on a well-floured.
2. Get each half of the dough, then roll it to make a loaf about 12 inches long in the shape of French bread. Place on a greased baking sheet and cover with a towel.
3. Let rise until doubled, about 1 hour—Preheat oven to 450 F (220 °C). Bake until golden brown, turning the pan around once halfway during baking. Transfer the loaves to a rack.

Nutrition:

Calories 201

Carbohydrates: 42 g

Fat 0.6 g

Protein 6 g

169. Italian Bread

This bread is at once crisp and chewy with a beautiful golden-brown crust.

Preparation time: 2 hours

Cooking time: 1 hour and 10 minutes

Servings: 2 loaves

Ingredients:

- 1 tablespoon of light brown sugar
- 4 cups all-purpose flour, unbleached
- 1 ½ teaspoon of salt
- 1 1/3 cups + 1 tablespoon warm water
- 1 package active dry yeast
- 1 ½ teaspoon of olive oil
- 1 egg
- 2 tablespoons cornmeal

Directions:

1. Place flour, brown sugar, 1/3 cup warm water, salt, olive oil, and yeast in your bread machine. Select the dough cycle. Hit the start button. Deflate your dough. Turn it on a floured surface. Form two loaves from the dough.
2. Keep them on your cutting board. The seam side should be down. Sprinkle some cornmeal on your board. Place a damp cloth on your loaves to cover them. Wait for 40 minutes. The volume should double.
3. In the meantime, preheat your oven to 190 °C. Beat a 1 tablespoon of water and an egg in a bowl. Brush this mixture on your loaves.
4. Make an extended cut at the center of your loaves with a knife. Shake your cutting board gently, making sure that the loaves do not stick.

Now slide your loaves on a baking sheet—Bake in your oven for about 35 minutes.

Nutrition:

Calories 105

Carbohydrates: 20.6 g

Fat 0.9 g

Protein 3.1 g

170. Portuguese Sweet Bread

This bread is super light, soft, and tender. This recipe works with any white, unenriched, all-purpose-flour-based bread mix.

Preparation time: 2 hours

Cooking time: 1 hour and 5 minutes

Servings: 1 loaf

Ingredients:

- 1 egg beaten
- 1 cup milk
- 1/3 cup sugar
- 2 tablespoons margarine
- 3 cups bread flour
- ¾ teaspoon salt
- 2 ½ teaspoons active dry yeast

Directions:

1. Place everything into your bread machine. Select the sweet bread setting. Hit the start button. Move the loaves to a rack for cooling once done.

Nutrition:

Calories 139 Carbohydrates: 24 g

Fat 8.3 g Protein 3 g

171. Pita Bread

Pita bread is a soft pillowy bun with a crisp outside and soft inside. It can be eaten with any type of meal.

Preparation time: 35 minutes

Cooking time: 20 minutes

Servings: 8 pcs

Ingredients:

- 3 cups of all-purpose flour
- 1 1/8 cups warm water
- 1 tablespoon of vegetable oil

- 1 teaspoon salt
- 1 ½ teaspoon active dry yeast
- 1 active teaspoon white sugar

Directions:

1. Place all the fixings in your bread pan. Select the dough setting. Hit the start button. The machine beeps after the dough rises adequately.
2. Turn the dough on a floured surface. Roll, then stretch the dough gently into a 12-inch rope. Cut into eight pieces with a knife. Now roll each piece into a ball. It should be smooth.
3. Roll each ball into a 7-inch circle. Keep covered with a towel on a floured top for 30 minutes for the pita to rise. It should get puffy slightly.
4. Preheat your oven to 260 degrees C. Keep the pitas on your wire cake rack. Transfer to the oven rack directly.
5. Bake the pitas for 5 minutes. They should be puffed. The top should start to brown. Take out from the oven. Keep the pitas immediately in a sealed paper bag. You can also cover using a damp kitchen towel.
6. Split the top edge or cut it into half once the pitas are soft. You can also have the whole pitas if you want.

Nutrition:

Calories 191

Carbohydrates: 37g

Fat 3g

Protein 5g

172. Syrian Bread

Syrian bread is delicious, a holy treat. It's not dense like western bread -- it's light, soft, and slightly spongy. The trick to baking it is keeping the dough moist while it is rising by covering it with a cloth. If you do this, you will have the best bread you've ever tasted.

Preparation time: 20 minutes

Cooking time: 20 minutes

Servings: 8 pcs

Ingredients:

- 2 tablespoons vegetable oil
- 1 cup of water
- 1 ½ teaspoons salt
- ½ teaspoon white sugar
- 1 ½ teaspoon active dry yeast
- 3 cups all-purpose flour

Directions:

1. Put everything in your bread machine pan. Select the dough cycle. Hit the start button. Preheat your oven to 475 degrees F. Turn to dough on a lightly floured surface once done. Divide it into eight equal pieces. Form them into rounds.
2. Take a damp cloth and cover the rounds with it. Now roll the dough

into flat thin circles. They should have a diameter of around 8 inches.
3. Cook in your preheated baking sheets until they are golden brown and puffed.

Nutrition: Calories 204 Carbohydrates: 36g

Fat 5g Protein 5g

173. Sour Cream Chive Bread

This bread is excellent for campfire additions like chevre, swiss, or gorgonzola. Experiment with different cheese types and seasonings for other flavors, like chilies, for instance.

Preparation time: 10 minutes

Cooking time: 3 hours

Servings: 1 loaf

Ingredients: 2/3 cup whole milk at 70°-80°)

- 1/4 cup water at 70°-80°
- 1/4 cup sour cream
- 2 tablespoons butter
- 1-1/2 teaspoons sugar
- 1-1/2 teaspoons salt
- 3 cups bread flour
- 1/8 teaspoon baking soda
- 1/4 cup minced chives
- 2-1/4 teaspoons active dry yeast

Directions:

1. Place all the fixings in the bread machine pan in the order suggested by the manufacturer. Select basic bread setting.
2. Choose crust color and loaf size if available. Bake according to bread machine directions. Check the dough after 5 minutes of mixing and add 1 or 2 tablespoons of water or flour if needed.

Nutrition: Calories 105 Fat 2g

Carbohydrate 18g Protein 4g

174. Swedish Cardamom Bread

It is made with lots of butter, which gives it a golden color and rich flavor. The cardamom is not overwhelming, yet you will detect its sweet taste.

Preparation time: 35 minutes

Cooking time: 15 minutes

Servings: 1 loaf

Ingredients:

- ¼ cup of sugar

- ¾ cup of warm milk
- ¾ teaspoon cardamom
- ½ teaspoon salt
- ¼ cup of softened butter
- 1 egg
- 2 ¼ teaspoons bread machine yeast
- 3 cups all-purpose flour
- 5 tablespoons milk for brushing
- 2 tablespoons sugar for sprinkling

Directions:

1. Put everything except milk for brushing and sugar for sprinkling in the pan of your bread machine.
2. Select the dough cycle. Hit the start button. You should have an elastic and smooth dough once the process is complete. It should be double in size.
3. Transfer to a lightly floured surface. Now divide into three balls, then set aside for 10 minutes. Roll all the balls into long ropes of around 14 inches.
4. Braid the shapes. Pinch ends under securely and keeps on a cookie sheet. You can also split your dough into 2 balls. Smooth them and keep on your bread pan.
5. Brush milk over the braid. Sprinkle sugar lightly. Now bake in your oven for 25 minutes at 375 degrees F (190 degrees C).
6. Take a foil and cover for the final 10 minutes. It's prevents over-browning. Transfer to your cooling rack.

Nutrition: Calories 135 Carbohydrates: 22g

Fat 7g Protein 3g

175. Ethiopian Milk and Honey Bread

Ethiopian Milk and Honey Bread is a tasty treat for breakfast, after a meal when you are having coffee or tea.

Preparation time: 2 hours

Cooking time: 1 hour and 15 minutes

Servings: 1 loaf

Ingredients: 3 tablespoons honey

- 1 cup + 1 tablespoon milk
- 3 cups bread flour
- 3 tablespoons melted butter
- 2 teaspoons active dry yeast
- 1 ½ teaspoons salt

Directions:

1. Add everything to the pan of your bread. Select the white bread or basic setting and the medium crust setting.
2. Hit the start button. Take out your hot loaf once it is done. Keep on your wire rack for cooling. Slice your bread once it is cold and serve.

Nutrition: Calories 129 Carbohydrates: 20 g

Fat 3.8 g Protein 2.4 g

176. Fiji Sweet Potato Bread

This bread is ideal for Buns. It is easy to make & tastes excellent even without the filling.

Preparation time: 2 hours

Cooking time: 1 hour and 10minutes

Servings: 1 loaf

Ingredients:

- 1 teaspoon vanilla extract
- ½ cup of warm water
- 4 cups flour
- 1 cup sweet mashed potatoes
- 2 tablespoons softened butter
- ½ teaspoon cinnamon
- 1 ½ teaspoons salt
- 1/3 cup brown sugar
- 2 tablespoons powdered milk
- 2 teaspoons yeast

Directions:

1. Add everything in the pan of your bread. Select the white bread and the crust you want. Hit the start button. Set aside on wire racks for cooling before slicing.

Nutrition:

Calories: 168 Cal

Carbohydrates: 28 g

Fat: 5g

Protein: 4 g

177. Italian Panettone

Italian Christmas cake is a great way to get family and friends to gather at your house during the holidays. Try it toasted with a smear of butter.

Preparation Time: 15 minutes

Cooking Time: 3 hours

Servings: 16

Ingredients:

- 3/4 cup warm water
- 4 large egg yolks
- 2 teaspoons vanilla extract
- 1/2 cup sugar

- 1 teaspoon lemon zest
- 1 teaspoon orange zest
- 1/2 teaspoon salt
- 1/2 cup of unsalted butter, cut into pieces
- 3 1/4 cups unbleached flour
- 1 package bread machine yeast
- 1/2 cup golden raisins
- 1/2 cup raisins
- 1 egg white, slightly beaten
- 4 sugar cubes, crushed

Directions:

1. Add the water, egg yolks, vanilla, and zest to the bread maker pan. Add the sugar, salt, and flour. Lay pieces of butter around the outside of the pan on top of the flour.
2. Press a well into the flour and add the yeast. Start the Dough cycle; at the second kneading cycle, add golden raisins and raisins. Let dough rise until doubled.
3. Prepare the baking case, cut a parchment paper circle to line the bottom of the 6-inch cake pan, and spray with non-stick cooking spray.
4. Separate another piece of parchment to line the inside of the brown paper bag after cutting the bag's bottom.
5. Fold the top edge down to form a cuff, then spray the inside of the parchment with cooking spray. Place the paper case in the pan.
6. Punch the dough down, then knead into a ball. Add it to the paper-lined pan case and allow it to rise until almost doubled.
7. Preheat the oven to 350°F. Baste the top of the panettone dough with the beaten egg white and sprinkle with the crushed sugar cubes.
8. Bake within 30 minutes, then reduce heat to 325°F and bake another 30 minutes. Remove from oven and cool in the pan for about 15 minutes, then cool on a rack until ready to serve.

Nutrition:

Calories: 201 Fat: 7.2 g

Carbs: 30.6 g Protein: 3.9 g

178. Bread of the Dead (Pan de Muertos)

A traditional cake served on All Souls Day, Bread of the Dead is delicious and should be consumed in memory of your loved ones.

Preparation Time: 5 minutes

Cooking Time: 2 hours 50 minutes

Servings: 12

Ingredients:

- 1/3 cup water
- 4 1/2 tablespoons butter
- 4 1/2 eggs

- 3/8 cup sugar
- 3/4 teaspoon salt
- 1/3 teaspoon orange zest
- 1/8 teaspoon star anise
- 2 1/3 cups bread flour
- 1 1/2 teaspoons bread machine yeast

Directions:

1. Mix the dry fixings and set aside. Add the liquid ingredients to the bread maker pan first, then gently pour the mixed dry ingredients on top of the liquid.
2. Set for Sweet bread cycle, medium crust color, and press Start. Transfer to a cooling rack within 20 minutes before slicing to serve.

Nutrition:

Calories: 162

Fat: 6.2 g

Carbs: 22.4 g

Protein: 4.4 g

179. Mexican Sweet Bread

While the precise origin of this bread is unknown, it is a Mexican treat you'll quickly fall in love with. Serve with a cup of Mexican hot chocolate for a satisfying snack on a cold day.

Preparation Time: 5 minutes

Cooking Time: 3 hours

Servings: 12

Ingredients:

- 1 cup whole milk
- 1/4 cup butter
- 1 egg
- 1/4 cup sugar
- 1 teaspoon salt
- 3 cups bread flour
- 1 1/2 teaspoons yeast

Directions:

1. Add wet ingredients to the bread maker pan. Add dry ingredients, except yeast. Make a well or a deep hole in the center of the dry fixings and add the yeast.
2. Set to Sweet Bread cycle, light crust color, and press Start. Remove to a cooling rack within 15 minutes before serving.

Nutrition:

Calories: 182

Fat: 5.2 g

Carbs: 29.2 g

Protein: 4.6 g

180. Challah

This loaf is unique Jewish bread and light and delicious on its own or topped with just about any spread!

Preparation Time: 15 minutes

Cooking Time: 1 hour 40 minutes

Servings: 12

Ingredients: 1/2 cup warm water

- 1 package active dry yeast
- 1 tablespoon sugar
- 3 tablespoons butter, softened
- 1/2 teaspoon kosher salt
- 2 to 2 1/2 cups kosher all-purpose flour - 2 eggs - 1 egg yolk
- 1 teaspoon water

Directions:
1. Add sugar and salt to the bread maker pan. Add butter, eggs, then water. Add flour and yeast. Select the Dough cycle and press Start.
2. Transfer dough to a large mixing bowl sprayed with non-stick cooking spray. Oiled dough using a non-stick cooking spray and cover. Let rise in a warm place within 45 minutes.
3. Punch dough down. Remove dough to lightly floured surface; pat dough and shape into a 10-by-6-inch rectangle. Divide into 3 equal strips with a pizza cutter. Braid strips and place into a 9-by-5-inch loaf pan sprayed with non-stick cooking spray. Wrap or cover, then let it rise in a warm area for about 30 to 45 minutes. Beat egg yolk with 1 teaspoon water and baste loaf. Bake at 375°F for 25 to 30 minutes, or until golden. Let cool on a rack within 5 minutes before removing from loaf pan and serve.

Nutrition: Calories: 64 Fat: 4 g

Carbs: 5.2 g Protein: 1.9 g

181. Russian Black Bread

A symbol of health and wealth, Russian black bread is best baked for times of celebration. It's also great as the base of Reuben sandwiches!

Preparation Time: 5 minutes

Cooking Time: 3 hours

Servings: 1

Ingredients: 1 1/4 cups dark rye flour

- 2 1/2 cups unbleached flour

- 1 teaspoon instant coffee
- 2 tablespoons unsweetened cocoa powder
- 1 tablespoon whole caraway seeds
- 1/2 teaspoon dried minced onion
- 1/2 teaspoon fennel seeds
- 1 teaspoon of sea salt
- 2 teaspoons active dry yeast
- 1 & 1/3 cups water - 1 teaspoon sugar
- 1 1/2 tablespoons dark molasses
- 1 1/2 tablespoons apple cider vinegar
- 3 tablespoons vegetable oil

Directions:

1. Mix dry fixings in a bowl, except for the yeast. Add wet ingredients to bread pan first; top with dry ingredients.
2. Make a well or a deep hole in the center of the dry ingredients and add the yeast. Select the Basic bread cycle, medium crust color, and press Start. Let cool for 15 minutes before slicing.

Nutrition: Calories: 169 Fat: 3.9 g

Carbs: 29.8 g Protein: 4.6 g

182. Russian Rye Bread

Slightly crumbly and tangy in taste, Russian Rye Bread is perfect for creamy dips or served toasted with sharp white cheddar cheese or labneh.

Preparation Time: 5 minutes

Cooking Time: 3 hours

Servings: 12

Ingredients:

- 1 1/4 cups warm water
- 1 3/4 cups rye flour
- 1 3/4 cups whole wheat flour
- 2 tablespoons malt (or beer kit mixture)
- 1 tablespoon molasses
- 2 tablespoons white vinegar
- 1 teaspoon salt
- 1/2 tablespoon coriander seeds
- 1/2 tablespoon caraway seeds
- 2 teaspoons active dry yeast

Directions:

1. Mix dry fixings in a bowl, except for the yeast. Add wet ingredients to bread pan first; top with dry ingredients.
2. Make a well in the center of the dry ingredients and add the yeast. Press Basic bread cycle, choose medium crust color and press Start.
3. Remove from the bread pan and allow to cool on a wire rack before serving.

Nutrition:

Calories: 141 Fat: 0.8 g

Carbs: 29.7 g Protein: 5 g

183. Portuguese Corn Bread

Cook up a traditional taste of Portugal with this decadent yet delicately sweet cornbread. Enjoy it with soups or buttered on its own.

Preparation Time: 8 minutes

Cooking Time: 2 hours

Servings: 8

Ingredients:

- 1 cup yellow cornmeal
- 1 1/4 cups cold water, divided
- 1 1/2 teaspoons active dry yeast
- 1 1/2 cups bread flour
- 2 teaspoons sugar
- 3/4 teaspoon salt
- 1 tablespoon olive oil

Directions:

1. Stir cornmeal into 3/4 cup of the cold water until lumps disappear. Add cornmeal mixture and oil to the bread maker pan.
2. Add remaining dry ingredients, except yeast, to the pan. Make a well in the center of the dry ingredients and add the yeast.
3. Choose a Sweetbread cycle, light crust color, and press Start. Transfer to a plate and serve warm.

Nutrition:

Calories: 108

Fat: 1.7 g

Carbs: 20.6 g

Protein: 2.6 g

184. Amish Wheat Bread

Amish Wheat Bread is simple, moist, and easy to make in no time. Serve this hearty loaf with your favorite soups and salads.

Preparation Time: 10 minutes

Cooking Time: 2 hours 50 minutes

Servings: 12

Ingredients:

- 1 1/8 cups warm water
- 1 package active dry yeast
- 2 3/4 cups wheat flour
- 1/2 teaspoon salt
- 1/3 cup sugar
- 1/4 cup canola oil
- 1 large egg

Directions:

1. Put warm water, sugar, plus yeast into the bread maker pan; let sit for 8

minutes or until it foams. Add remaining ingredients to the pan.
2. Select the Basic bread cycle, light crust color, and press Start. Transfer to a cooling rack within 20 minutes before slicing.

Nutrition: Calories: 173 Fat: 5.3 g

Carbs: 27.7 g Protein: 3.7 g

185. British Hot Cross Buns

Bake a taste of Britain with these delicious buns traditionally eaten at Easter. Be sure to serve them warm with a cup of English Breakfast tea and a spot of milk.

Preparation Time: 20 minutes

Cooking Time: 2 hours 30 minutes

Servings: 12

Ingredients:

- 3/4 cup warm milk
- 3 tablespoons butter, unsalted
- 1/4 cup white sugar
- 1/2 teaspoon salt
- 1 egg
- 1 egg white
- 3 cups all-purpose flour
- 1 tablespoon active dry yeast
- 3/4 cup dried raisins
- 1 teaspoon ground cinnamon

For Brushing:

- 1 egg yolk
- 2 tablespoons water

For the Crosses:

- 2 tablespoons flour
- Coldwater
- 1/2 tablespoon sugar

Directions:

1. Put milk, butter, 1/4 cup sugar, salt, egg, egg white, flour, and yeast in the bread maker and start the Dough cycle. Add raisins and cinnamon 5 minutes before the kneading cycle ends.
2. Allow resting in the machine until doubled, about 30 minutes. Punch down on a floured surface, cover, and let rest 10 minutes.
3. Shape into 12 balls and place in a greased 9-by-12-inch pan. Cover and let rise in a warm place until doubled, about 35-40 minutes.
4. Mix egg yolk and 2 tablespoons water and baste each bun. Mix the cross ingredients to form pastry. Roll out the pastry and cut into thin strips. Place across the buns to form crosses.
5. Bake at 375°F for 20 minutes. Remove from pan immediately and cool on a rack. Serve warm.

Nutrition:

Calories: 200 Fat: 4 g

Carbs: 36.5 g Protein: 5.2 g

186. Hawaiian Bread

Sweet Hawaiian bread is out of this world! This bread makes delicious sandwiches and even French toast.

Preparation Time: 5 minutes

Cooking Time: 3 hours

Servings: 12

Ingredients:

- 3/4 cup pineapple juice
- 1 egg
- 2 tablespoons olive oil
- 2 tablespoons whole milk
- 2 1/2 tablespoons sugar
- 3/4 teaspoon salt
- 3 cups bread flour
- 1 1/2 teaspoons active dry yeast

Directions:

1. Add the wet fixings to the bread maker pan, then add sugar, salt, and flour. Make a well or a deep hole in the center of the dry ingredients and add the yeast
2. Press Basic bread cycle, choose medium crust color and press Start. Remove from the bread pan and allow to cool before serving.

Nutrition:

Calories: 160 Fat: 3.1 g

Carbs: 28.7 g Protein: 4 g

187. Greek Easter Bread

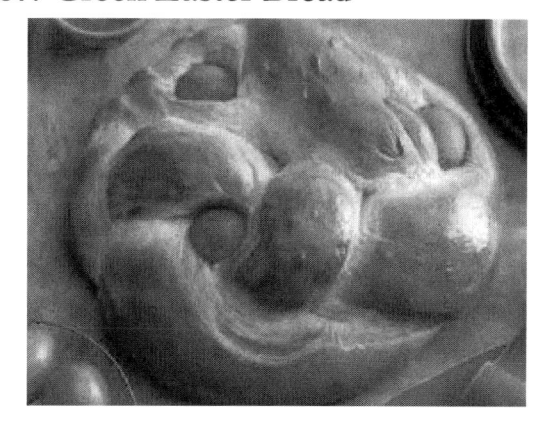

Tsoureki is a traditional bread served at Easter in Greece. You'll love this quick and easy way to bake this traditional holiday bread.

Preparation Time: 20 minutes

Cooking Time: 3 hours

Servings: 12

Ingredients:

- 2/3 cup fresh butter
- 1 cup milk
- 1 cup of sugar
- 1 teaspoon mastic
- 1/2 teaspoon salt
- 1 package active dry yeast
- 3 eggs
- 5 cups strong yellow flour

- 1 egg, for brushing blended with 1 teaspoon water

Directions:

1. Heat milk and butter until melted in a saucepan; do not boil. Add to bread maker pan. Add sugar and mastic to a food processor and blend; add to bread maker pan. Add remaining ingredients.
2. Set the Dough cycle and press Start; leave the dough to rise one hour after the process. Shape into 2 loaves, cover, and leave to rise for 50 more minutes. Baste with egg wash.
3. Bake at 320°F for 30 to 40 minutes or until golden brown. Transfer to a cooling rack for 15 minutes before serving.

Nutrition:

Calories: 554 Fat: 12.9 g

Carbs: 97.6 g Protein: 13.4 g

188. Sweet Potato Bread with Honey

Sweet potato bread with honey is hearty and dense. Best served with savory meats, you'll love this satisfying and nourishing taste.

Preparation Time: 5 minutes

Cooking Time: 3 hours

Servings: 12

Ingredients:

- 1 1/4 cups sweet potato, mashed
- 10 tablespoons canned coconut milk
- 1 teaspoon ginger, fresh grated
- 1 tablespoon lemon zest
- 2 tablespoons honey
- 2 tablespoons olive oil
- 3 cups bread flour
- 1 teaspoon salt
- 2 1/4 teaspoons rapid-rise yeast

Directions:

1. Add the wet fixings to the bread maker pan. Mix dry fixings, except for yeast, in a bowl. Add to pan. Make a well or a deep hole in the center of the dry ingredients and add the yeast.
2. Press Basic bread cycle, choose medium crust color and press Start. Remove from the bread pan and allow to cool before serving.

Nutrition:

Calories: 193

Fat: 5.5 g

Carbs: 32.2 g

Protein: 4.2 g

189. Za'atar Bread

Whip up a taste of the Middle East with this delicious and perfectly seasoned bread. Serve with hummus and your favorite kebabs.

Preparation Time: 5 minutes

Cooking Time: 3 hours

Servings: 12 – 14

Ingredients:

- 1/3 cup za'atar seasoning
- 2 tablespoons onion powder
- 1 cup of warm water
- 2 tablespoons agave nectar
- 1/4 cup applesauce
- 3 cups bread flour
- 1 teaspoon salt
- 2 1/4 teaspoons rapid-rise yeast

Directions:

1. Mix dry fixings in a bowl, except for the yeast. Add wet ingredients to bread pan first; top with dry ingredients.
2. Make a well in the center of the dry ingredients and add the yeast. Press Basic bread cycle, choose medium crust color and press Start.
3. Remove from the bread pan and allow to cool before serving.

Nutrition:

Calories: 125

Fat: 1.2 g

Carbs: 24.6 g

Protein: 4.1 g

190. Bread Machine Pizza Dough

Bread Machine Pizza Dough is one of the recipes that will work great in a bread machine. Furthermore, you can prepare it faster and easier with a bread machine.

Preparation time: 10 minutes

Cooking time: 20 min

Servings: 2 12" pizzas

Ingredients:

- 1 cup + 2 tbsp of water
- 2 tbsp of olive oil/vegetable oil
- 3 cups bread flour
- 1 tsp of granulated sugar

- 1 tsp of salt
- 2 1/2 tsp of active dry yeast or bread machine yeast

Directions:

1. Place all ingredients in bread pan in the order specified. Choose the dough process. Move the rack from the oven to the lowest location and preheat to 400 degrees. Grease 2 pizza plates or sheets of cookies. When done, split the dough into two.
2. Place each half with floured fingers into a 12 "circle. Top with your favorite toppings. Let the bread cook for 15 to 20 minutes, or until the crust is light brown.

Nutrition:

Calories: 130

Carbs: 24g

Fat: 1g

Protein: 5g

191. Perfect Thin Crust Pizza Dough

Perfect Thin Crust Pizza Dough is precisely what it is called- perfect. It is a healthy pizza crust recipe that can be made humongous and thin, or it can be made smaller to make about 4 personal sized pizzas.

Preparation Time: 15 minutes

Cooking Time: 20 minutes

Servings: 3

Ingredients:

- 3/4 to 1 cup of lukewarm water (110 degrees F.)
- 1 tablespoon of olive oil, extra virgin
- 1 teaspoon of coarse salt
- 1 1/2 teaspoon of granulated sugar
- 3 cups of bread flour
- 2 teaspoons of instantly active dry yeast

Directions:

1. In the bread machine pan, add all the dough ingredients (in the order listed). Process to dough setting according to the manufacturer's instructions.
2. After completing the dough process, remove the dough from the pan and place it in a lightly oiled bowl. Cover, and let the dough rise slowly in the refrigerator for 24 hours before using.

Nutrition:

Calories: 189

Carbs: 42g

Fat: 1g

Protein: 0g

192. Pizza Crust

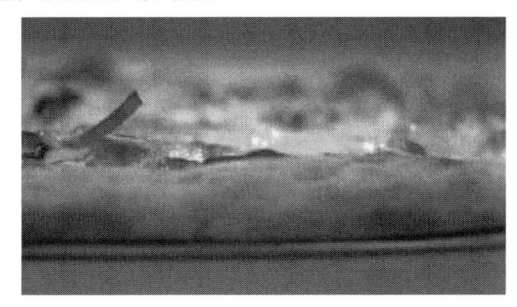

Pizza Crust is a convenient way to make a pizza on a weeknight. Place in the bread machine and go. Be careful about attempting to eat it straight off the machine.

Preparation time: 15 minutes

Cooking Time: 2 hours & 5 minutes

Servings: 10

Ingredients:

- 3/4 cup water
- 1 tablespoon of vegetable oil
- 1 teaspoon of lemon juice
- 1/2 teaspoon of salt
- 1 tablespoon of white sugar
- 1 tablespoon of dry milk powder
- 2 1/4 cups of bread flour
- 1 teaspoon of active dry yeast

Directions:

1. Put all ingredients in the pan of the bread machine, in the manufacturer's suggested order. Select Cycle for Dough; press Start. After the rise cycle, remove the dough from the pan and use it for your favorite pizza recipe.

Nutrition: Calories: 170 Carbs: 27g

Fat: 5g Protein: 4g

193. Rustic Pizza Bread

Rustic Pizza Bread is a wonderfully quick and moist bread to make.

Preparation Time: 15 minutes

Cooking Time: 2 hours

Servings: (1 Loaf) 14 Slices

Ingredients:

- 2 tbsp olive oil
- 2 tbsp raw honey
- 1 tsp fine sea salt
- 3 1/4 cups white entire-wheat flour + for dusting extra
- 1 tbsp vital wheat gluten
- 2 1/2 tsp instant or bread maker yeast
- 1 1/2 tsp garlic powder
- 2 tbsp partitioned dried oregano
- 3 oz sundried-tomatoes, chopped
- 1/2 cup black chopped olives, pitted
- 3/4 cup part-skim mozzarella cheese, shredded
- 1 egg white, beaten
- 2 tsp sesame seeds

Directions:

2. In a bread machine, put 1 1/4 cups of oil, water, honey, salt, gluten, flour, garlic powder, yeast, and

oregano 1 tbsp according to the manufacturer's direction.
3. Program bread maker for setting "dough." Upon completion of the dough process, move to work surface the dough with flour-dusted lightly.
4. The dough in a rectangle shape is about as wide and long as the bread maker, around 10-12 inches. Sprinkle the dough generously with olives, tomatoes, mozzarella, and 1 tbsp of oregano left over.
5. Roll dough, jelly-roll style, starting on one of the short sides, to form a log shape. Remove the paddle from the baking pan of the bread machine and put the dough log in the pan to ensure that on the bottom is the seam. The pan is placed back in the bread maker and allow the loaf to rise for 1 hr.
6. Brush the top gently with a white egg, and then sprinkle it with sesame seeds once the loaf has risen. Set bread machine cycle "Bake-only" for 1 hour and 20 minutes.
7. After 1 hour, check the bread. Bread is made when on top, it is slightly golden, and it has a hollow appearance.
8. Immediately remove from the pan, and before slicing, allow to cool. Cooled bread is kept for 2 to 3 days refrigerated or at room temperature, securely wrapped in plastic.

Nutrition:

Calories: 310 Carbs: 44g

Fat: 11g Protein: 8g

194. Red Pesto Focaccia

Both the dough and the pesto in this lively, ruby-hued loaf contain sun-dried tomatoes. It's essential to buy the kind that comes packed in oil since it is also an ingredient in the pesto.

Preparation time: 30 minutes

Cooking time: 15 minutes

Servings: 6-8

Ingredients:

For the dough:

- 1¼ teaspoons yeast
- 2½ cups all-purpose flour
- 1 teaspoon salt
- 1 teaspoon sugar
- 4 to 5 oil-packed sun-dried tomatoes, drained
- 1 cup of water

For the red pesto:

- 6 garlic cloves
- 15 oil-packed sun-dried tomatoes, plus 2 tablespoons of the oil
- 2 teaspoons dried rosemary leaves

- ¼ teaspoon freshly ground black pepper
- Pinch of salt

To finish the focaccia:

- 3 tablespoons olive oil

Directions:

1. Place all fixings in the machine, set for Dough, Basic Dough, or Manual, and press Start. If the dough appears sticky, add up to 1/3 cup additional flour, 1 tablespoon at a time. While the dough is rising, you can prepare the Red Pesto.
2. For the red pesto, place all the ingredients in a food processor and process for 10 to 15 seconds. The red pesto should be coarse and not smooth, so be careful that you do not over process.
3. Warm oven to 450°F with the rack in the center position, brush the olive oil over a heavy cookie sheet and set it aside.
4. Move the dough to a lightly floured work surface and let it rest for 5 minutes. Rol-out your dough to a 12-inch circle and transfer it to the prepared cookie sheet.
5. Spread the pesto over the surface of the dough. Bake the focaccia for 15 minutes, or until it is crisp and golden brown, then cut in wedges and serve hot or warm.

Nutrition:

Calories: 100 Carbs: 18g

Fat: 2g

Protein: 3g

195. Hummus Focaccia

Toasted chickpea flour mix with light whole wheat flour gives this flatbread a wholesome nutty taste. Sesame seeds, ground (tahini), and whole add sweetness and crunch.

Preparation time: 45 minutes

Cooking time: 24 minutes

Servings: 8-10

Ingredients:

For the dough:

- 1 tablespoon yeast
- 1 cup toasted chickpea flour
- 1 cup White Wheat flour
- 1 cup all-purpose flour
- 1½ teaspoons salt
- ½ teaspoon garlic powder
- ½ teaspoon coarsely ground black pepper
- 1/3 cup tahini
- 1 extra-large egg
- ¾ cup plus 2 tablespoons water or more to serve a slightly sticky dough

To finish the focaccia:

- 1 egg beaten with 1 tablespoon water
- 3 tablespoons sesame seeds

Directions:

1. Place all the dough fixings in the machine, program for Manual or Dough, and press Start. This dough is sticky but should form a discrete ball. If it's dry and crumbly after the first 3 minutes of kneading, add 1 to 2 additional tablespoons of water.

2. When it's done, use your hands or a rolling pin to form the dough into a 9-inch disk. Brush the top with half of the egg glaze and then sprinkle it liberally with sesame seeds.
3. Drizzle the remaining half of the egg glaze over the sesame seeds. Put the dough, uncovered, in a warm place to rise until almost doubled in bulk, 30 to 40 minutes.
4. Warm-up the oven to 425°F with the rack in the center position, then before you place the dough in the oven, gently press the surface with your fingertips to make light indentations.
5. Bake the focaccia for 20 to 24 minutes until the underside is lightly colored and the sesame seeds are golden brown. Serve hot or at room temperature.

Nutrition:

Calories: 117 Carbs: 14g

Fat: 5g Protein: 3g

196. Porcini Focaccia

If you love the dark, deep-woods flavor of porcini mushrooms, then this double-barrel loaf is for you. It's a glorious deep mushroom color, perfumed with porcini, and set off by tiny flashes of caraway. The inside is moist and tender, and the top is lightly crusted with coarse salt.

Preparation time: 2 hours

Cooking time: 25 minutes

Servings: 8

Ingredients:

For the dough:

- 1 ounce (¾ cup) dried porcini mushrooms
- 1¾ cups boiling water
- 1 tablespoon yeast
- 2 cups less 2 tablespoons all-purpose flour
- 1 cup whole wheat flour
- 2 tablespoons buckwheat flour
- 1/3 cup cornmeal
- 1½ teaspoons salt
- 1 tablespoon sugar
- 1 teaspoon coarsely ground black pepper
- 1/3 cup porcini oil
- 1 tablespoon caraway seeds

To finish the focaccia:

- 2 tablespoons porcini oil
- 2 teaspoons coarse salt

Directions:

1. Put the mushrooms in a small bowl, soak them with the boiling water for 10 to 15 minutes, or until they are very soft.
2. Set a fine-mesh sieve over a glass 2-cup measure and drain off the liquid,

pressing the mushrooms gently to squeeze out as much excess liquid as possible. Reserve the liquid.

3. Place all the dough fixings and 1 cup of the reserved mushroom liquid in the machine, program for Dough or Manual, and press Start.
4. At the end of the final knead, form the dough into a 9-inch round and place it on a baking sheet or pizza pan lightly dusted with cornmeal.
5. Cover it with a clean cloth and allow the dough to rise in a warm place until almost doubled in bulk. It will take about 1 hour because buckwheat and whole wheat flour have very little gluten.
6. Preheat the oven to 425°F with the rack in the center position. Use your fingertips to make light indentations on the top of the dough.
7. Drizzle the top with the oil and sprinkle with the salt. Bake within 20 to 25 minutes, or until the top is deep brown and the underside is dry and browned as well. Serve hot or at room temperature.

Nutrition:Calories: 174 Carbs: 5g

Fat: 15g Protein: 6g

197. Potato Caraway Focaccia

This soft-crusted, mellow high-rising loaf looks and tastes like a work of art. A slight hint of cumin brings a golden taste to the velvety soft crumb.

Preparation time: 35 minutes

Cooking time: 17 minutes

Servings: 8-10

Ingredients:

For the dough:

- 2½ teaspoons yeast
- 1½ teaspoons salt
- 1 cup rye flour
- 2 cups all-purpose flour
- ½ teaspoon ground cumin
- ½ teaspoon freshly ground black pepper
- 1 cup (8 ounces) mashed potatoes made from scratch
- ¼ cup garlic oil or olive oil
- 2/3 cup water

To finish the focaccia:

- 2 tablespoons olive oil
- 1 tablespoon caraway seeds

Directions:

1. Put all fixings in the machine, program for Dough or Manual, and press Start.
2. Do not add more water until the potatoes give up their cooking liquid—about 5 minutes into the first kneading cycle.
3. Then add just enough to make a firm ball. At the end of the final cycle, remove the dough, which will be

quite tacky and soft, to a lightly floured workspace.

4. Sprinkle the dough with flour and knead briefly by hand, adding only enough flour to form a soft ball of dough.
5. Place the dough ball either on a wooden pizza paddle sprinkled with cornmeal or on a cornmeal-dusted baking sheet. Cover with a clean cloth and let the dough rise for 30 minutes in a warm place.
6. Preheat the oven to 450°F with either the rack or a pizza stone or tiles in the center position. Before placing the dough in the oven, indent the top of it with your fingertips, pushing down rather aggressively to deflate it, not entirely but by about a third.
7. Drizzle it with the olive oil, then sprinkle with the caraway seeds. Slide the pan into the oven or the dough onto the pizza stone or tiles.
8. Bake for 10 minutes at 450°F, then lower the oven to 375°F and bake an additional 5 to 7 minutes, or until the top is deep golden brown and the bottom is browned as well. Serve hot, warm, or at room temperature.

Nutrition:

Calories: 150

Carbs: 17g

Fat: 6g

Protein: 6g

198. Rosemary Mustard Focaccia

Grainy mustard lends a distinctive flavor to this fragrant loaf. Try to use fresh rosemary when available since the taste is far superior to dried, and the leaf-studded focaccia is so pretty.

Preparation time: 15 minutes

Cooking time: 20 minutes

Servings: 6-8

Ingredients:

For the dough:

- 1 tablespoon yeast
- 1 cup White Wheat flour
- 2 cups all-purpose flour
- 1/3 cup yellow cornmeal
- 2 teaspoons salt
- ¼ cup olive oil
- 1 cup water, plus an additional 1 to 2 tablespoons if necessary
- 1/3 cup grainy mustard
- ¼ cup fresh rosemary leaves or 1½ tablespoons dried rosemary

Directions:

1. Place all the dough fixings in the machine, program for Dough or Manual, and press Start. Add just

enough extra water until the dough forms a relaxed yet discrete ball.

2. When it's finished, shape your dough into a 10-inch disk. Place it either on a pizza peel or baking sheet that has been sprinkled with cornmeal. Cover the dough with a clean cloth and allow it to rise in a warm place until doubled in bulk.
3. Warm the oven to 450°F with the rack or a pizza stone in the center position. Just before baking, use your fingertips to make ½-inch dimples in the top of the dough.
4. Slide the pan into your oven, bake for 17 to 20 minutes, or until crusty and golden brown. Cool the focaccia slightly before cutting it into wedges.

Nutrition:

Calories: 160

Carbs: 31g

Fat: 2g

Protein: 6g

199. Green Peppercorn Focaccia

Want spice-up to your life? Wait until you see how adding a few tables- spoons of green peppercorns to simple focaccia can jazz things up. Great on its own and extraordinary when split and slathered with goat cheese, this green peppercorn focaccia stands out from the rest.

Preparation time: 1 hour & 15 minutes

Cooking time: 15 minutes

Servings: 8-10

Ingredients:

For the dough:

- 1 tablespoon yeast
- 1 cup whole wheat flour
- 2 cups all-purpose flour
- 3 tablespoons cornmeal
- 1½ teaspoons salt
- 1¼ cups water
- 3 tablespoons garlic oil or 3 tablespoons olive oil plus 1 large garlic clove, minced
- 2 tablespoons green peppercorns, drained of brine

To finish the focaccia:

- 2 tablespoons olive oil or garlic oil
- Coarse salt
- Freshly ground black pepper

Directions:

1. Place all the dough fixings in the machine except the peppercorns, set for Dough or Manual, and press Start.
2. When it's done, add the peppercorns and restart the machine, kneading

just until the peppercorns are incorporated but not pulverized.
3. Form the dough into a 10-inch disk. Place it either on a pizza peel that has been dusted with cornmeal. Allow the dough to rise, uncovered, for 1 hour in a warm place.
4. Warm the oven to 475°F with the rack or a pizza stone in the center position. Just before baking, use your fingertips to make indentations in the surface of the dough.
5. Drizzle using the oil, then sprinkle with salt and pepper—Bake for 15 minutes, or until well browned. Enjoy hot, warm, or at room temperature.

Nutrition:

Calories: 174

Carbs: 5g

Fat: 15g

Protein: 6g

200. Roasted Garlic and Olive Focaccia

This focaccia is for serious garlic and olive lovers! An excellent item to keep around the kitchen is a bottle of olive oil infused with fresh rosemary and garlic, which is very special for making any focaccia or pizza.

Preparation time: 20 minutes

Cooking time: 20 minutes

Servings: 8-10

Ingredients:

For the dough:

- 1¼ teaspoons yeast
- 2 cups all-purpose flour
- ½ teaspoon salt
- 3/4 cup water
- 2 tablespoons olive oil

To finish the focaccia:

- 2 tablespoons olive oil
- Salt to taste
- Freshly ground black pepper to taste
- 12 garlic cloves, roasted
- ½ cup pitted olives: black colossal, green Spanish, Kalamata, or Italian or Greek
- oil-cured

Directions:

1. Put all the dough fixings in the machine, program for Dough, Basic Dough, or Manual, and press Start.
2. Preheat the oven to 400°F. When it's done, transfer the dough to a lightly floured working surface and let it rest for 5 minutes.
3. Roll the dough into a 10-inch circle, then transfer it to a lightly floured cookie sheet. Brush the surface of

the dough with olive oil and then sprinkle with the salt and pepper.
4. Layout the garlic and olives over the top and let the dough rise for an additional 5 minutes—Bake within 20 minutes, or until lightly browned. Serve hot, warm, or at room temperature, cut into wedges.

Nutrition:

Calories: 286

Carbs: 48g

Fat: 7g

Protein: 9g

Conclusion

Thanks for making it to the end of this guide. Bread is considered as the basic necessity for survival in life. Everyone consumes the bread according to his or her own choices and preferences. It is also observed that bread is preferred over any other food item. Variation in the bread-making occurs from country to country as well. The key ingredients in bread making are flour, yeast, oil, water, salt, sugar, milk, and eggs; they impart different and unique characteristics. Even the quantity of these key ingredients can primarily affect the end product. Over the past few years, advancements in technology have made home chores easier, making kitchen work easy to handle. One such innovation is that of a bread maker.

A bread maker or bread machine is a home-made bread making appliance. Bread has also been consumed and all sorts of food, making it essential in all meals, whether it be breakfast, lunch, or dinner. While baking results may vary considerably from one bread machine to the other, the flavor of bread baked in a device is opposite from that of bread baked in the oven, even if the same recipe is used. Besides, bread maker bread has a heavier and more dense consistency rather than lightweight and airy.

Bread machines are getting popular day by day due to their level of convenience in use. Considering the convenience of using bread machines, it is suggested that they are user-friendly, which means that it can be dealt with; with great ease. It also gives the user opportunity to experiment and explore different ingredients and types of bread in their home comfort. It provides the consumer with freshly baked bread whenever needed.

While people love home-baked bread, some individuals don't like the smoothness of bread baked in a device and often ignore a bread maker's convenience to produce bread. The machine does all the kneading work on the dough system, which helps it go through the initial cycles of rising and rest. It does not only save energy, but it also causes a less baking mess. The dough and the basic white bread recipes can make the sweet dough, pizza dough, and cinnamon bunks for some options.

Launching and finishing a bread in a bread machine yields better results with less time than mixing by hand. Whenever the dough cycle completes, you create it for the second time and allow it to rise—Bake as you wish in the oven. You may concentrate your attention on certain household activities or meal chores when the dough is in the process using a bread machine. And it helps you to perform multiple tasks in a sense.

A bread machine has many benefits over conventional bread baking and purchasing the pre-packed loaves at a store. Sometimes, this is cheaper. The machines are very user friendly. You ought to be precise with the proportions.

Without a bread maker, you can undoubtedly make traditional bread, but this machine can be convenient for cleaning and preparing. You can control your bread recipes, so it is easy to adapt the recipes or ingredients accordingly if you would like gluten-free flour or lowered salt. But as gluten makes the standard bread texture, you have to ensure that you have the right gluten-free flour and that your bread maker is "gluten-free" to be perfectly baked.

If you try to reduce palm oil, making bread on your own is an excellent way to do that, as many shops purchased bread contain palm oil. If you bake regularly, then buying a bread machine makes absolute sense. The gadget can make both mixing and kneading the dough simple for you. Moreover, the celebrations, occasions, and other festivals are incomplete without the bread. A variety of ingredients are added according to the occasion as well as season.

Some of the problems with bread machines are shape issues in which the final product is asymmetrical and not enough spongy and fluffy. Issues with the texture include bread being denser, having many holes, and not wholly baked in a given time. Careful handling of ingredients measurement and following the suggested order for the ingredients can reduce the chances of getting a faulty loaf of bread. Cautious handling of ingredients measurement and following the suggested order for the ingredients can reduce the chances of getting a defective loaf of bread.

With all that said, it can be assumed that the bread machine would save you a lot of time and energy to knead the dough you'd put in, and you would need less workforce, too, if you own a venture. Hence, it's economical as well.

Recipes Index

#

3-Seed Bread

A

Alligator Animal Italian Bread

Almond Chocolate Chip Bread

Almond Meal Bread

American Cheese Beer Bread

Amish Bread

Amish Wheat Bread

Apricot Oat Bread

Aromatic Lavender Bread

B

Bacon and Walnuts Rye Bread

Bacon Jalapeño Cheesy Bread

Banana Chocolate Chip Bread

Barley Bread

Basic Rye Bread

Basic Rosemary Bread

Basic White Bread

Basil and Sundried Tomato Bread

Baxis White Bread

Beef and Parmesan Bread

Beetroot Prune Bread

Best Bread Machine Bread

Bran Packed Healthy Bread

Bread Machine Multigrain Loaf

Bread Machine Pizza Dough

Bread of the Dead (Pan de Muertos)

Bread with Beef and Hazelnuts

Bread with Chicken, Apricots, and Raisins

Bread with Ham and Sausages

Bread with Sausages and Celery

Breakfast, Fruit and Chocolate Bread Part

Breakfast, Fruit and Chocolate Bread Part

Breakfast, Fruit and Chocolate Bread Part

British Hot Cross Buns

Broccoli and Cauliflower Bread

Butter Bread Rolls

Butter Honey Wheat Bread

Buttermilk Honey Bread

Buttermilk Rye Bread

Buttermilk Wheat Bread

Buttermilk White Bread

C

Cajun Bread

Caraway Rye Bread

Carrot Oat Bread

Cauliflower and Garlic Bread

Chai Cake

Challah

THE BREAD MACHINE COOKBOOK FOR BEGINNERS:

Cheese Blend Bread

Cheese Bread

Cheese Jalapeno Bread

Cheese Spinach Crackers

Cheesy Garlic Bread

Cheesy Keto Sesame Bread

Chicken Bread

Chocolate Cherry Bread

Chocolate Chip Bread

Chocolate Orange Bread

Cinnamon & Dried Fruits Bread

Cinnamon Bread

Cinnamon Swirl Bread

Cinnamon-Raisin Bread

Corn, Poppy Seeds and Sour Cream Bread

Cottage Cheese Bread

Cracked Black Pepper Bread

Cracked Wheat Bread

Cranberry & Golden Raisin Bread

Cranberry Orange Breakfast Bread

Cream Cheese Bread

Cream Cheese Rolls

Crunchy Wheat Herbed Bread

Cumin Bread

Cumin Tossed Fancy Bread

Curd Bread

Curd Onion Bread with Sesame Seeds

Curvy Carrot Bread

D

Danish Rugbrod

Danish Spiced Rye Bread

Dark Rye Loaf

Dill and Cheddar Bread

E

Easy Gluten-Free, Dairy-Free Bread

Eight-Grain Bread

English Muffin Bread

Ethiopian Milk and Honey Bread

European Black Bread

F

Fiji Sweet Potato Bread

Flax and Sunflower Seed Bread

Flower Power Bread

French Baguettes

French Cheese Onion Bread

French Ham Bread

G

Garlic, Herb and Cheese Bread

German Pumpernickel Bread

Gluten-Free Brown Bread

Gluten-Free Chia Bread

Gluten-Free Cinnamon Raisin Bread

Gluten-Free Crusty Boule Bread

Gluten-Free Oat & Honey Bread

Gluten-Free Paleo Bread

Gluten-Free Pizza Crust

Gluten-Free Potato Bread

Gluten-Free Pull-Apart Rolls

Gluten-Free Pumpkin Pie Bread

Gluten-Free Simple Sandwich Bread

Gluten-Free Sorghum Bread Recipe

Gluten-Free Sourdough Bread

Gluten-Free Whole Grain Bread

Golden Corn Bread

Golden Potato Bread

Grampy's Special Bread

Greek Easter Bread

Green Peppercorn Focaccia

H

Hawaiian Bread

Health Dynamics Rye Bread

Healthy Celery Loaf

Herbal Garlic Cream Cheese Delight

High Flavor Bran Bread

Homemade Wonderful Bread

Honey and Flaxseed Bread

Honey Lavender Bread

Honey White Bread

Honey Whole Wheat Bread

Hummus Focaccia

I

Italian Bread

Italian Onion Bread

Italian Panettone

J

Jos Rosemary Bread

L

Lavender Buttermilk Bread

Lemon Poppy Seed Bread

Light Oat Bread

M

Macadamia Nut Bread

Maple Whole Wheat Bread

Mexican Chocolate Bread

Mexican Sweet Bread

Montana Russian Black Bread

Multigrain Bread with Honey

Multigrain Raisin Bread

Multi-Seed Bread

Mustard Wheat Rye Sandwich Bread

N

New York Rye Bread

Nutty Bread

O

Oat and Honey Bread

Oat Bread

Oatmeal Bread

Olive Bread with Italian Herbs

Onion Bacon Bread

Onion Bread

Onion Potato Bread

Orange Walnut Candied Loaf

Orchard's Dream Bread

Oregano Mozza-Cheese Bread

Original Italian Herb Bread

P

Paradise Bread

Parmesan Italian Bread

Peanut Butter Bread

Perfect Thin Crust Pizza Dough

Pita Bread

Pizza Crust

Porcini Focaccia

Portuguese Corn Bread

Portuguese Sweet Bread

Potato Bread

Potato Caraway Focaccia

Potato Rosemary Bread with Honey

Potato Rosemary Loaf

R

Red Pesto Focaccia

Rice Bread

Ricotta Bread

Roasted Garlic and Olive Focaccia

Rosemary & Garlic Coconut Flour Bread

Rosemary Cranberry Pecan Bread

Rosemary Mustard Focaccia

Russian Black Bread

Russian Rye Bread

Rustic Pizza Bread

Rye Bread

S

Saffron Tomato Bread

Savory Breads

Selecting the Right Kind of Yeast

Sesame and Flax Seed Bread

Sesame French Bread

Sesame Seeds & Onion Bread

Seven Grain Bread II

Seven-Grain Bread

Seven-Grain Millet Bread

Seven-Grain Oat Molasses Bread

Sour Cream Chieve Bread

Spent Grain Wheat Bread

Spiced Cauliflower Buns

Spinach Bread

Sun Vegetable Bread

Sunny Delight Loaf

Swedish Cardamom Bread

Sweet Potato Bread with Honey

Syrian Bread

T

Ten Grain Bread

Tomato Bread

Tomato Onion Bread

Turkey Breast Bread

Turmeric Bread

W

Walnut Bread

Walnut Cocoa Bread

White Bread

Whole Wheat Breakfast Bread

Wholegrain Bread

Whole-Grain Sesame Bread

Whole-Wheat Bread

Y

Yeasted Cornbread

Z

Za'atar Bread

Zucchini Carrot Bread

Zucchini Herbed Bread

Printed in Great Britain
by Amazon